PATHS TO PEACE

PATHS TO PEACE

A Collection of Prayers, Ceremonies and
Chants
from Many Traditions

Compiled and Edited
by
John Matthews

CHARLES E. TUTTLE COMPANY
Boston • Rutland, Vermont • Tokyo

First published in the United States in 1992 by
Charles E. Tuttle Company, Inc. of Rutland, Vermont & Tokyo, Japan,
with editorial offices at 77 Central Street, Boston, Massachusetts 02109.

Library of Congress Catalog Card Number 92-61202
ISBN 0-8048-1818-5

A portion of the royalties from this volume
is devoted to the support of children in need.

Cover design by Gary Fujiwara
Text typeset by Tek Art Ltd.
PRINTED IN THE UNITED STATES

To All Our Children

CONTENTS

INTRODUCTION

During the Gulf Crisis I became aware that a great number of people from every walk of life and connected with many faiths and disciplines were actively working to bring an end to the war. These people were neither part of the military nor, in many instances, were they representatives of any established religious body. For the most part, they were ordinary men and women who deplored the waste and needless violence of the war, and who sought, by other means, to bring the conflict to a conclusion.

In many cases, these people did no more than take part in an increasingly active prayer life, which they adhered to every day that the crisis lasted. Others sought a more direct approach, devising ceremonies or rituals designed to combat war by enabling them to enter into an inner part of themselves where hostile things remain unknown.

As I became aware of all this activity, I began consciously to seek it out and to take part myself wherever I could. It became obvious that similar 'spiritual activists' existed everywhere and were perpetually engaged in a global resistance to the many conflicts which seem to break out almost daily somewhere in the world.

Then I recalled other, earlier, times when Britain had been at war or even threatened with invasion, and sought, through the exercise of spiritual strength, to turn back the enemy. In Celtic mythology I found the story of Bran the Blessed who, when he knew himself to be mortally wounded, commanded his followers to cut off his head and bury it facing out to sea; for, as long as it remained there, no invasion could take place. (Later the hero Arthur had it dug up, in the belief that he alone should guard the land.)

At the time of the Spanish Armada in 1588, English wise women and men gathered together on the cliffs along the south coast in order to call up a storm to drive the Spanish fleet far off course and hinder the invasion of England.

During the Second World War not only did the opposing sides employ powerful esoteric experts to aid them, but once again the witches of Britain came to their country's assistance, using natural forces to help keep Hitler's fleet penned up along the shores of

France until the tide of war turned against it. In this instance, many of the older members of the hidden esoteric community voluntarily sacrificed themselves – going out into the woods to die so that their spiritual power would be released and could become activated in the cause of peace.

Throughout history numerous individuals have devoted themselves to the quest for peace, and of these a high proportion have based their approach on the practice of spiritual principles. A prime example is Mahatma Gandhi, the great Indian leader, who promulgated a doctrine of non-violence. Centuries earlier Gautama Buddha, after seven years of isolation, during which time he struggled with the demons of pain, fear and hatred, found his way to the heart of peace. While in the West the entire Quaker movement, founded by George Fox in 1668, has devoted itself to the promotion of peace through spiritual means.

The tradition of spiritual peace-work is thus well established. Frequently uncoordinated, spontaneous, yet ultimately effective, this work is in progress even as I write, and will certainly keep going for as long as it is needed. The present book is but a tiny indication of the richness and variety of the activities being undertaken; and it is a tribute to the many ways in which the contributors, known and unknown, responded and continue to respond to the growing need of their fellow human beings for peace.

This book is not simply a collection of rituals or ceremonies. It contains prayers, invocations, seed thoughts, poems and a selection of more general writings on the theme of peace. It is these which delineate the many paths to peace, pursued by all who seek a better world and a better life, who care about the future of our race and our planet.

For, of course, peace concerns far more than global conflict. War can be just as prevalent in ghettos around the world, in city streets and in quiet country lanes, as in battlefields. It is present in the home life and work place of many of us, and within the spirits of far more individuals than we can ever know. This book encompasses ways to peace in these situations too: there are seed thoughts upon which to meditate, prayers to utter, blessings to give, mantras to chant, songs to sing, ceremonies of sacred peace to perform in the home as well as in the synagogue, church or mosque.

Many of the greatest thinkers and some of the most enlightened people who have ever lived are quoted here. Many other contributors are anonymous, or unknown to the world at large. But they all share a desire to see an end to the ever-present threat of war – war which may blot out everything, the good along with the bad.

The revealed faiths of Buddhism, Christianity, Islam and Judaism are represented, as are the older beliefs of the native traditions – of North America, Britain and Ireland – which share similar approaches to the question of peace. Whatever their affiliation, the voices which speak to us from these pages possess a unity which transcends creed or culture. They are quiet voices, but they speak with power and they speak with love.

These pages contain honest responses to a frightening reality; all are written from the heart, sometimes with not a little degree of personal pain. To read them is to be moved – as I have frequently been while working on the compilation of this book – but it is also to be inspired, as I hope all who read them will be. For here is a call that cannot be denied if the human race is to survive the next millennium, so soon to dawn. Such work as may be found within this book is only a beginning: when you come to read the blessings, prayers and invocations (many to unfamiliar goddesses and gods), perceptions of your own will start to form – ideas for ways in which you too can follow one of the paths to peace, such as by devising your own ceremony or meditation. If enough people do this, we may yet turn back the rising tide of fear, greed, hatred and doubt which creeps up on us day by day.

In the words of the great native American wisdom-speaker Black Elk:

> We shall burn the sweet grass as an offering to *Wakan-Tanka* [the Supreme Being], and the fragrance of this will spread throughout heaven and earth; it will make the four-leggeds, the wingeds, the star peoples of the heavens, and all things as relatives. From you, O Grandmother Earth, who are lowly, and who support us as does a mother, this fragrance will go forth; may its power be felt throughout the universe, and may it purify the feet and hands of the two-leggeds, that they may walk forward upon the sacred earth, raising their heads to *Wakan-Tanka*.

JOHN MATTHEWS
Oxford, 1991

CHAPTER ONE

PRAYERS AND BLESSINGS
(Calling upon the Many Names of Deity)

Man prays, and prayer fashions man. The saint has himself become prayer, the meeting place of earth and heaven: he thus contains the universe, and the universe prays with him. FRITHJOF SCHUON

Prayer is a means of talking to deity. It may be rehearsed in the inner sanctum of the brain, or uttered more formally before the shrine of a chosen goddess or god. More, it is a way of formulating a thought so that it is both compact and forceful. The drawing up of words from the depths of the soul and aiming them towards the infinite realms is itself a kind of magical act.

The power and effectiveness of prayer have long been recognised in every corner of the world. Within the Christian tradition (specifically Greek and Russian Orthodox) whole books of instruction have been based around the Jesus Prayer: 'Lord Jesus Christ, Son of God, have mercy upon me'. In a tradition which goes back to the monks of Mount Athos and beyond to the Desert Fathers in the first century AD, these words were spoken or chanted aloud continuously, whilst being meditated upon. The following instruction from the writings of Bishop Ignatius Brianchinov gives some idea of how this works:

> You are aware that our breathing by which we live is an inhaling and exhaling of air. The organs that serve for this purpose are the lungs which surround the heart. They pass air through themselves and flood the heart with it. Thus breathing is the natural way to the heart. And so, collect your mind and conduct it by way of your breathing by which air passes to the heart and, together with the inhaled air, force it to descend into the heart and stay there. And train it not to come out of there quickly; for at this inner enclosure, restraint is very wearisome, but when it becomes accustomed to it, then on the contrary it does not like whirling without, because it is therefore filled with joy and happiness . . .
>
> When you enter the place of the heart as I have shown you, give thanks to God and, while glorifying His goodness, always maintain this activity; it will teach you what you will never learn in any other way.

Ignatius of Loyola (1491–1566) the founder of the Jesuit Order, also composed a treatise of spiritual instruction (*The Spiritual Exercises*) in which the importance of prayer is emphasised. Later, in 1657, the mystic Angelus Silesius wrote in his work *The Cherubic Wanderer* (I.237):

> Man, if thou wishest to know what it is to pray sincerely,
> Enter into thyself, and interrogate the Spirit of God.

Turning to the East, we have the words of the Muslim Ibn Ata'illah (written *circa* 1250):

> Prayer is a cleansing for hearts from the strain of iniquities, and an opening of the door of the Mysteries.
> Prayer is the place of confidence and the wellspring of intimacies: in it widens the scope of the Mysteries, and in it shine the rays of the luminaries.

In this chapter there are contributions from many traditions, beginning with a beautiful piece by the anonymous author of the Hermetic texts and ending with José Arguëlles's 'Prayer of the Seven Galactic Directions'. Here is a Druidic prayer, a prayer to the Great Mother, a Vedic hymn, a prayer to Nārāyanī, and a Native American prayer to the Great Spirit. Here, too, are blessings, themselves a form of prayer whereby the protection of the deity is summoned and sealed upon and around the subject or object to be blessed. Foremost among the blessings included in this section are those from the Celtic tradition, which seem to capture the very essence of prayer, both as supplication and solemn vow.

Be aware, too, that you can make your own prayers and blessings, which will be every bit as valid as any that you have read here. There is perhaps no more perfect way to create a path to peace than by formulating a prayer of your own, for it is at once a ritual, a meditation and a cry from the heart. If sufficient people make petition to the deity, in time Creation itself, however we personify it, must surely hear.

Let every bar of the universe be flung open to me;
and let all nature receive the sound of my hymn.
Be thou opened, O Earth, and ye trees, wave not your boughs;
I am about to sing the praise of Him who is both the All and the
One.
Be ye opened, ye heavens, and ye winds, be still;
let the immortal sphere of heaven receive my utterance.
For I am about to sing the praise of Him who created all things,
who fixed the earth, and hung heaven above;
who made the sweet water flow from Ocean into the lands wherein
men dwell,
that it might serve for the sustenance of all mankind,
and gave command that fire should come forth,
to be used by gods and men in all their works.
Let us all with one accord give praise to Him,
who is seated high upon the heavens, creator of all that is.
It is He that is the eye of my mind;
may He accept the praise sung by my Powers.
Ye Powers that are within me, praise ye the One and the All;
sing ye in concord with my will, all ye Powers that are within me.
O holy Knowledge, by thee am I illumined,
and through thee do I sing praise to the incorporeal Light.
. . . I rejoice in joy of mind;
rejoice with me, all ye Powers.
O Good that is in me, praise the Good;
O Life and Light, from you comes the song of praise, and to you
does it go forth.
I give thanks to thee, O Father, who workest in my Powers;
I give thanks to thee, O God . . .
Thus crying, the Powers that are in me accomplish thy will;
praising the All, they fulil thy purpose.
It is thy Word that through me sings thy praise;
for by thee, O Mind, is my speech shepherded.
Through me accept from all an offering of speech;
for the All is from thee, and to thee returns the All.
O Light, illumine thou the mind that is in us;
O Life, keep my soul alive.
Thy man cries thus to thee by means of the things thou hast made;
but he has got from thine eternity the praises which he utters.
I have seen that which I seek;
I have found rest according to thy purpose;
by thy will I am born again.

HERMES TRISMEGISTUS

The Mantram of Unification

The sons of men are one and I am one with them.
I seek to love, not hate;
I seek to serve, not exact due service
I seek to heal, not hurt.

Let pain bring due reward of light and love.
Let the soul control the outer form, and life and all events
And bring to light the love that underlies the happenings of the
    time.

Let vision come and insight.
Let the future stand revealed.
Letter inner union demonstrate and outer cleavages be gone.
Let love prevail.
Let all men love.

                                        ALICE A. BAILEY

Our Mother, thou who art in the darkness of the underworld,
May the memory of the holiness of thy name shine forth,
May the breath of the awakening of thy kingdom warm the hearts
    of all homeless wanderers,
May the resurrection of thy will enliven eternal faithfulness even
    unto the depths of corporeal substance.
Receive this day the living rememberance of thee from human
    hearts,
Who implore thee to forgive the debt of forgetting thee,
And are ready to fight against the temptation in the world which
    has led thee to existence in the darkness,
That through the Deed of the Son the immeasurable pain of the
    Father be stilled,
Through the freeing of all beings from the tragedy of thy
    withdrawal.
For thine is the homeland, and the all-bestowing greatness, and the
    all-merciful grace, for all and everything in the circle of
    all.   Amen.

                                Twentieth-century prayer, Anon.

Prayer to the Great Spirit

O great spirit
Whose voice I hear in the wind
Whose breath gives life to the world
Hear me
I come to ask you as one of your many children
I am small and weak
I need your strength and wisdom
May I walk in beauty
Make my eyes behold the red-and-purple sunset
Make my hands respect the things that you have made
     and my ears sharp to hear your voice
Make me wise so that I may know
     the things that you have taught your children
     the lessons that you have hidden in every leaf and rock
Make me strong
Not to be superior to my brothers
But to be able to fight my greatest enemy – myself
Make me ever ready to come to you with straight eyes
So that when life fades as the faded sunset
My spirit will come to you without shame

Traditional Native American

Prayer of the Great Goddess

May the Great Goddess watch over all peoples and bring them to the flowering of their fulfilment. May She nourish and protect them, who are all, unknowing, Her Children.

May She bring to them the knowledge of their fellowship within Her hall, in which all races live, of their companionship at Her table, from which all nations eat.

May all the men and women of Earth take up the stewardship of their inheritance. May joy and fulfilment come to those who care for this bright globe; may understanding come to those who labour unaware.

Let the grace of the Goddess be born within us all, the children of Earth and Heaven. Let the knowledge of Her fellowship guide our actions and our lives.

PRUDENCE JONES

Druid Prayer

Deep within the still centre of my being
    may I find peace.
Silently within the quiet of the Grove
    may we share peace.
Gently within the greater circle of humankind
    may we radiate peace.

CHRISTINE WORTHINGTON

Lord, may I sleep in peace and wake up to a good life. Cover me with the shelter of Your peace and protect me because You are good.

A Jewish child's prayer

Blessing of the Goddess Badb

Peace up to heaven
Heaven down to earth,
Earth under heaven,
Strength in every one.

Traditional Gaelic

Lead us from darkness to Light.
Lead us from the unreal to the Real.
Lead us from death to Immortality.
Lead us from chaos to Beauty.

ALICE A. BAILEY

O thou that makest wars to cease in all the world in accordance
with thine ancient name: we beseech thee to make war and tumult
now to cease. From the murmer and subtlety with which we view
one another give us rest. Make a new beginning, and mingle again
the kindred of nations in the alchemy of love, and with some finer
essence of forbearance and forgiveness temper our minds.

ARISTOPHANES

Prayer to Nārāyanī

Salutation, O Nārāyanī.
Thine is the power of creation, preservation and dissolution.
Thou art eternal. Thou art the Ground of Being.
Thou art the energies of Nature.

Salutation, O Nārāyanī.
Thou who workest the salvation of those in suffering and distress
who take refuge in Thee.
Thou, O Devī, who removes the sufferings of all . . .

Who is there but Thyself in sciences,
in the Scriptures, and in the Vedic sayings
that light the lamp of understanding.

O Queen of the universe, protector of the universe, support of the
universe.
Thou art the goddess worthy to be adored by the Lord of the
universe.
Those who bow to Thee in devotion become the refuge of the
universe.

O Devī, be Thou please, and grant us protection from the fear of
foes forever,
as Thou hast protected us now by the destruction of the asuras.
Destroy the sins of the worlds and the great calamities that have
arisen through the maturing of evil portents.

Traditional Indian Prayer

Loving Kindness

May every creature abound in well-being and peace.
May every living being, weak or strong, the long and the small
The short and the medium-sized, the mean and the great
May every living being, seen or unseen, those dwelling far off,
Those near by, those already born, those waiting to be born
May all attain inward peace

Let no one deceive another
Let no one despise another in any situation
Let no one, from antipathy or hatred, wish evil to anyone at all.
Just as a mother, with her own life, protects her only son from hurt
So within yourself foster a limitless concern for every living
        creature.
Display a heart of boundless love for all the world
In all its height and depth and broad extent
Love unrestrained, without hate or enmity.
Then as you stand or walk, sit or lie, until overcome by drowsiness
Devote your mind entirely to this, it is known as living here life
        divine.

Buddhist Prayer

Prayer to Rudra

Father of the Maruts, send your kindness here. Do not cut us off from the sight of the sun. Let the hero spare our horses. O Rudra, let us be born again through our children.

By those most healing medicines that you give, Rudra, I would attain a hundred winters. Drive hatred far away from us, and anguish farther away; drive diseases away in all directions.

Of what is born, you, Rudra, are the most glorious in glory, the strongest of the strong, with the thunderbolt in your hand. Carry us safely to the farther shore of anguish; ward off all attacks or injury.

We would not wish to anger you, Rudra the bull, by acts of homage or ill praise, or by invoking you together with another god. Raise up our heroes with your healing medicines; I hear that of all healers you are the best healer.

Rig Veda

Pray for the Children

Oh Great Mystery, Creator of life,
We ask that our lives may be
Walks of beauty and balance,
For all the world to see.
Gently we'll walk on Mother Earth,
Respecting her Sacred Space,
In order to nurture the future,
For the children of every race.
May we dream the abundance
Of the worlds yet to come,
Never wasting our blessings,
But gathering, for generations yet unborn.
Teach us how to rid ourselves,
Of the enemies who live within,
The jealousies, fears, and hatreds
That keep us from being friends.
Sacred Mystery, hear our prayer,
As we hold our hearts up high,
We cry for the waking dream to emerge,
So like Eagle,
            loving freedom,
                        we may fly.

JAMIE SAMS/MIDNIGHT SONG

Peace be to earth and to airy space!
Peace be to heaven, peace to the waters,
Peace to thē plant and peace to the trees!
May all the powers grant to me peace!
By this invocation of peace may peace be diffused!
By this invocation of peace may peace bring peace!
With this peace the dreadful I now appease,
With this peace the cruel I now appease,
With this peace all evil I now appease,
So that peace may prevail, happiness prevail!
May everything for us be peaceful!

Atharva Veda, XIX

Petition

Be Thou a smooth way before me,
Be Thou a guiding star above me,
Be Thou a keen eye behind me,
This day, this night, for ever.

I am weary, and I forlorn,
Lead Thou me to the land of the angels;
Methinks it were time I went for a space
To the court of Christ, to the peace of heaven;

If only Thou, O God of life,
Be at peace with me, be my support,
Be to me as a star, be to me as a helm,
From my lying down in peace to my rising anew.

Traditional Gaelic

Lord, make me an instrument of your peace:
where there is hatred, let me sow love;
where there is injury, pardon;
where there is doubt, faith;
where there is despair, hope;
where there is darkness, light;
where there is sadness, joy.
O Divine Master, grant that I may not so much
seek to be consoled as to console;
to be understood, as to understand;
to be loved as to love.
For it is in giving that we receive,
it is pardoning that we are pardoned,
and it in dying that we are born to eternal life.

ST FRANCIS OF ASSISI

Grant me thy grace, most merciful Jesus, that it may be with me, and may labour with me, and continue with me to the end . . .

Let Thy will be mine, and let my will always follow Thine, and agree perfectly therewith . . .

Grant that I may rest in Thee above all things that can be desired, and that my heart may be at peace in Thee.

Thou are the true peace of the heart, Thou art its only rest; out of Thee all things are irksome and restless.

In this very peace which is in Thee, the one Supreme Eternal Good, I will sleep and take my rest.

THOMAS À KEMPIS

Autumn Psalm of Fearlessness

I am surrounded by a peaceful ebbing,
    as creation bows to the mystery of life;
    all that grows and lives must give up life,
    yet it does not really die.
As plants surrender their life,
    bending, brown and wrinkled,
    and yellow leaves of trees
    float to my lawn like parachute troops,
    they do so in a sea of serenity.

I hear no fearful cries from creation,
    no screams of terror,
    as death daily devours
    once-green and growing life.
Peaceful and calm is autumn's swan song,
    for she understands
    that hidden in winter's death-grip
    is spring's openhanded,
    full-brimmed breath of life.

It is not a death rattle that sounds
    over fields and backyard fences;
    rather I hear a lullaby
    softly swaying upon the autumn wind.
Sleep in peace, all that lives;
    slumber secure, all that is dying,
    for in every fall there is the rise
    whose sister's name is spring.

EDWARD HAYS

God of our Father,
great and merciful God.
Lord of peace and life.
Father of all.

You have plans of peace, and not of affliction.
You condemn wars
and defeat the pride of the violent.

You sent your Son Jesus
to preach peace to those who are near and far away,
to gather people of every race and nation
into a single family.

Hear the single-hearted cry of your children,
the anguished plea of all humanity:
no more war, a spiral of death and violence;
put an end to . . . war . . .
a threat against all your creatures
in heaven, on the earth and in the sea.

In communion with Mary, the Mother of Jesus,
once again we implore you:

speak to the hearts of those responsible
for the fate of peoples,
stop the 'logic' of revenge and retaliation;
with your Spirit suggest new solutions,
generous and honourable gestures,
room for dialogue and patient waiting,
which are more fruitful than the hurried deadlines of war.

Give our era days of peace.
War no more. Amen.

POPE JOHN PAUL II

A Litany for Peace

From organised and orchestrated hate,
Blind prejudice, refusals to relate;
Deliver us before it is too late:
We beseech thee to hear us, good Lord.

That archetypal images, invoked, inflamed
When subject peoples seek identity, be named,
May be fulfilled and quieted, and passions tamed:
We beseech thee to hear us, good Lord.

And save us from conventions, deeply drilled,
Dehumanising rivals, freely willed,
That they – not being human – may be killed!
We beseech thee to hear us, good Lord.

From turning our religions into god,
Pronouncing others evil, bad, or odd;
From righteousness imposed by iron rod:
We beseech thee to hear us, good Lord.

Rid all the world of Empires, large and small,
That long-subjected peoples may walk tall
And, free at last to live and be, may give their all:
We beseech thee to hear us, good Lord.

ANTHONY DUNCAN

Lord, put thou my tears in thy sight and my hearty prayer fully come into heaven to thee.

Lead me forth into the path of light, into the dearest country of men living, set me in the siker rest-folds of thy flocks, which art a good shepherd, which again-seekest and again-leadest things lost, defendest and savest things found, nourishest and makest whole sick things.

And thou art merciful, Lord, which confoundest not men hoping in thee, forsakest not men again-seeking thee, puttest not men away, again-turning to thee, but receivest in full-out joying and praising, and grantest to reign everlastingly in bliss together with thy saints and with thy chosen. For one Godhead, glory, virtue, honour, empire and power be to thee with the Father everlasting and Holy Ghost, into worlds of worlds. Amen.

Pseudo-Augustine

Prayer for Peace of the Heart

Most sacred, most loving Heart of Jesus,
hidden in the Holy Eucharist,
you beat for us still.
You say, as you said when you lived,
'My delight is to be with the children of men.'

When you come to live within me,
make my heart beat with your Heart:
make my soul free from all that is earthly,
all that is hard and cruel,
all that is proud and sensual,
all baldness, disorder and death.

Fill my heart with your presence,
so that nothing can disturb me,
but that in your love and your fear,
I may have peace.

CARDINAL NEWMAN

A Psalm of Benediction

Elizabeth Blessed be Shaddai forever!
She has visited Her people.
She liberates us
and through us liberates
all of Her sons and daughters.

Zechariah We are saved from all who would harm us,
as promised by the prophets
and a covenant of mercy,
so that we might serve Her
fearlessly
in holiness
and in justice
every day,
all the days of our life.

Elizabeth You, little child, are the prophet
called to prepare Her ways.
Go before Her.
Reveal Her wisdom.
Extend Her tender mercies
with the dawn of this new day,
so that all who sit in the shade of oppression
may walk in the light of One Who guides
our feet on the paths
of peace.

MIRIAM THERESE WINTER

The Affirmation of the Disciple

I am a point of light within a greater Light.
I am a strand of loving energy within the stream of Love divine.
I am a point of sacrificial Fire, focussed within the fiery Will of
    God.
    And thus I stand.

I am a way by which men may achieve.
I am a source of strength, enabling them to stand.
I am a beam of light, shining upon their way.
    And thus I stand.

And standing thus, revolve
And tread this way the ways of men,
And know the ways of God.
    And thus I stand.

ALICE A. BAILEY

Deep peace of the running wave to you,
of water flowing, rising and falling,
sometimes advancing, sometimes receding . . .
May the stream of your life flow unimpeded!
Deep peace of the running wave to you!

Deep peace of the flowing air to you,
which fans your face on a sultry day,
the air which you breathe deeply, rhythmically,
which imparts to you energy, consciousness, life.
Deep peace of the flowing air to you!

Deep peace of the quiet earth to you,
who, herself unmoving, harbours the movements
and facilitates the life of the ten thousand creatures,
while resting contented, stable, tranquil.
Deep peace of the quiet earth to you!

Deep peace of the shining stars to you,
which stay invisible till darkness falls
and disclose their pure and shining presence,
beaming down in compassion on our turning world.
Deep peace of the shining stars to you!

Deep peace of the watching shepherds to you,
of unpretentious folk who, watching and waiting,
spend long hours out on the hillside,
expecting in simplicity some Coming of the Lord.
Deep peace of the watching shepherds to you!

Deep peace of the Son of Peace to you,
who, swift as the wave and pervasive as the air,
quiet as the earth and shining like a star,
breathes into us His Peace and His Spirit.
Deep peace of the Son of Peace to you!

MARY ROGERS, adapted from the Gaelic

The peace of God be to you,
The peace of Christ be to you,
The peace of Spirit be to you
    And to your children,
    To you and to your children.

Traditional Gaelic

May the blessing of light be on you, light without and light within. May the blessed sunshine shine on you and warm your heart till it glows like a great peat fire, so that the stranger may come and warm himself at it, and also a friend.

And may the light shine out of the two eyes of you, like a candle set in the two windows of a house, bidding the wanderer come in out of the storm; and may the blessings of the rain be on you – the soft, sweet rain. May it fall upon your spirit so that all the little flowers may spring up and shed their sweetness on the air. And may the blessings of the Great Rains be on you, may they beat upon your spirit and wash it fair and clean, and leave there many a shining pool where the blue of heaven shines, and sometimes a star.

And may the blessing of the Earth be on you – the great round earth; may you ever have a kindly greeting for those you pass as you're going along the roads. May the earth be soft under you when you rest upon it, tired at the end of a day, and may it rest easy over you when at the last, you lay out under it; may it rest so lightly over you that your soul may be off from under it quickly and up and off, and on its way to God. And now may the Lord bless you and bless you kindly.

Traditional Irish

Peace between neighbours,
Peace between kindred,
Peace between lovers,
In love of the King of life.

Peace between person and person,
Peace between wife and husband,
Peace between women and children,
The peace of Christ above all peace.

Bless, O Christ, my face,
    Let my face bless everything;
Bless, O Christ, mine eye,
    Let mine eye bless all it sees.

Traditional Gaelic

The peace of joys,
The peace of lights,
The peace of consolations.

The peace of souls,
The peace of heaven,
The peace of virgins.

The peace of the fairy bowers,
The peace of peacefulness,
The peace of everlasting.

Traditional Gaelic

Blessing for a House

The peace of God, the peace of men,
The peace of Columba kindly,
The peace of Mary mild, the loving,
The peace of Christ, King of tenderness,
   The peace of Christ, King of tenderness,

Be upon each window, upon each door,
Upon each hole that lets in light,
Upon the four corners of my house,
Upon the four corners of my bed,
   Upon the four corners of my bed;

Upon each thing my eye takes in,
Upon each thing my mouth takes in,
Upon my body that is of earth
And upon my soul that came from on high,
   Upon my body that is of earth
   And upon my soul that came from on high.

Traditional Gaelic

The Vision of Enoch
(Arranged for a wedding ceremony)

I speak to you.
Be still
Know
I am
God.

I spoke to you
When you were born.
Be still
Know
I am
God.

I spoke to you
At your first sight.
Be still
Know
I am . . .

I spoke to you
At your first word.
Be still
Know
I am
God.

I spoke to you
At your first thought.
Be still
Know
I am . . .

I spoke to you.
At your first love.
Be still
Know
I am
God.

I spoke to you
At your first song.
Be still
Know
I am . . .

I speak to you
Through the grass of the meadows.
Be still
Know
I am
God.

I speak to you
Through the trees of the forests.
Be still
Know
I am . . .

I speak to you
Through the valleys and the hills.
Be still
Know
I am
God

I speak to you
Through the Holy Mountains.
Be still
Know
I am . . .

I speak to you
Through the rain and the snow.
Be still
Know
I am
God.

I speak to you
Through the waves of the sea.
Be still
Know
I am . . .

I speak to you
Through the dew of the morning.
Be still
Know
I am
God.

I speak to you
Through the peace of the evening.
Be still
Know
I am . . .

I speak to you
Through the splendor of the sun.
Be still
Know
I am
God.

I speak to you
Through the brilliant stars.
Be still
Know
I am . . .

I speak to you
Through the storm and the clouds.
Be still
Know
I am
God.

I speak to you
Through the thunder and lightning.
Be still
Know
I am . . .

I speak to you
Through the mysterious rainbow.
Be still
Know
I am
God.

I speak to you
When you are alone.
Be still
Know
I am . . .

I speak to you
Through the Wisdom of the Ancients
Be still
Know
I am
God.

I speak to you
At the end of time.
Be still
Know
I am . . .

I speak to you
When you have seen my Angels.
Be still
Know
I am
God.

I speak to you
Throughout Eternity.
Be still
Know
I am . . .

I speak to you
Be still
Know
I am
God.

Adapted from *The Gospel of the Essenes*

I choose the way of the interpreter, and therefore ask for light.
I choose the way of loving guidance, and therefore ask for lifting
power.
I choose the way of inspiration, and therefore ask for flowing life.
I choose the way of integrating, and therefore ask for the seal of
silence.

ALICE A. BAILEY

A Benediction at the End of a Prayer Time

O God of kindness and compassion,
    I have come to the conclusion
    of this time of prayer and worship,
    mindful of my position as your priestly servant.

I throw wide open the windows of my heart
    so that the peace of your presence
    may pour out in all four directions,
    showering its blessing upon all the earth.

May this benediction heal the wounds of war,
    bind up the bitterness of painful divisions
    and mend broken hearts and failed friendships,

As the blessing of your presence encircles the earth,
    may it awaken in all people
    a great desire to serve one another
    in humble and loving ways.
May it call proud hearts to gentleness
    and awaken the child in those
    who seek to hold power over others.

Inflame those hearts that have grown cold;
    reawaken within the weary of soul
    your spirits of youthfulness and joy.
Stir up your breath of freshness and enthusiasm
    that slumbers in tired hearts.

May this blessing flow forth from my heart,
    in your holy and infinite Name,
    in the redeeming name of your Son
    and in the living presence of the Holy Spirit.

    Amen+

EDWARD HAYS

Prayer of the Seven Galactic Directions

From the East House of Light
May wisdom dawn in us
So we may see all things in clarity

From the North House of Night
May wisdom ripen in us
So we may know all from within

From the West House of Transformation
May wisdom be transformed into right action
So we may do what must be done

From the South House of the Eternal Sun
May the right action reap the harvest
So we may enjoy the fruits of planetary being

From Above House of Heaven
Where star people and ancestors gather
May their blessings come to us now

From Below House of Earth
May the heartbeat of her crystal core
Bless us with harmonies to end all war

From the Center Galactic Source
Which is everywhere at once
May everything be known as the light of mutual love

OH YUM HUNAB K'U
EVAM MAY E MA HO!

JOSÉ ARGUËLLES

CHAPTER TWO

SEED THOUGHTS

(Points of Light in the Great Darkness)

Silence is the garden of meditation

'ALÎ (IBN ABÛ TÂLIB)

Thinking of peace, whether in abstract, cosmic, global or personal terms, can very easily lead to a blank wall. What *can* we do ourselves to usher in a new age of peaceful co-existence with our family, friends, neighbours, other nations, other species? All too often the answer is either not forthcoming, or else so huge and complex in its ramifications that we stand aghast before it.

One way to avoid this kind of stalled awareness is by meditation. Here, and in Chapter 6, 'Gleanings', are a number of brief seed thoughts from some of the great spiritual beings who have walked on this planet. From the words of Mahatma Gandhi to those of Lao Tzu, from the advice of Philo the Egyptian to that of the Native American medicine man Black Elk, the thoughts expressed here are often the distillation of a lifetime of meditation and pondering.

Our part is to work with these ideas, to broaden and deepen them through our own meditation. Simply by holding one of these thoughts in your mind throughout a single day, you will discover new things of which you were unaware. Take this seed thought from the *Dhammapada*: 'Better than a thousand useless words is one single word that gives peace.' The mere act of concentrating upon it has a profound effect, not only upon the individual who is meditating, but upon others with whom he or she comes into contact.

Meditation is one of the primary paths to peace. As the great contemporary spiritual teach Swami Sivananda (Sarasvati) explains in his *Practice of Meditation*:

> Meditation . . . is the path which leads to divinity. It is the Royal way to the kingdom of Brahman: it is the mysterious ladder which goes from earth to heaven, from error to truth, from darkness to light, from grief to joy, from restlessness to peace, from ignorance to knowledge, from death to immortality. Meditation leads us towards knowledge of the Self, that is to say, towards eternal peace and supreme felicity.

It is the achievement of this inner peace that is every bit as important as the more concrete aim of bringing about a worldwide cessation of hostilities. And, as with the prayers that began this book, the extracts that follow are only a brief selection of the words on the subject. You yourself should seek to add to them, to find your own seed thoughts, your own points of light in the great darkness in which we so often (rightly or wrongly) seem to dwell.

If we are to attain real peace in this world, we will have to begin with the children.

MAHATMA GANDHI

The stillness of a stone in a stream of truth.

PHILIP LE GALOISE

All Crises are a process of healing.

Anon.

I embrace the war within myself and I embrace all conflict within the human family. I breath peace and I breathe healing: in myself and in all others.

Anon.

Let us not demonise our enemies, but rather pray that the divine spirit wakes from sleep within them. Let resourceful compassion rule our every action that the circle of protection be maintained.

CAITLÍN MATTHEWS

The dream of peace is not enough. It can only be realised through the active operation of the heart.

JOHN MATTHEWS

There is light and love and divine power in everything.

Anon.

I see the possibility of a better game than war.

ROBERT FULLER

God is peace, His name is peace, and all is bound together in peace.

Zohar

Better than a thousand useless words is one single word that gives peace.

Dhammapada

'What is the best thing of all for a man, that he may ask from the Gods?'
'That he may always be at peace with himself.'

Contest of Homer and Hesiod

The peace of God, which passeth all understanding, shall keep your hearts and minds.

Philippians, 4:7

'Peace be with you' was the salutation of him who was the salvation of man. For it was meet that the supreme saviour should utter the supreme salutation.

DANTE ALIGHIERI

Having this knowledge [of the imperishable *Atma*], having become calm, subdued, quiet, patiently enduring, and collected, one sees the self in self.

Brihad-Aranyaka Upanishad, iv.iv.23

My peace I give unto you; not as the world giveth, give I unto you.

St John, 14:27

Peace is in that heart in which no wave of desire of any kind rises.

SWAMI RAMDAS

A peaceful mind is your most precious capital.

SWAMI SIVANANDA

No one has ever attained to the grandeur of glory
Of the soul which had established repose in its heart.

ANGELUS SILESIUS

There is nowhere perfect rest save in a heart detached.

MEISTER ECKHART

Verily in the remembrance of Allah do hearts find rest.

Qur'ân, xiii.82

In the Godhead may be no travail.

DAME JULIAN OF NORWICH

In peace is My dwelling place.

HELEN SUSO

God, that primitive unity, is that which is the alone original and fountain of all peace, and the centre of rest.

JOHN SMITH THE PLATONIST

Take no heed of time, nor of right or wrong. But passing into the realm of the Infinite, take your final rest therein.

CHUANG-TSE

Shall I not inform you of a better act than fasting, alms, and prayers? Making peace between one another: enmity and malice tear up heavenly rewards by the roots.

MUHAMMAD

Blessed are the peacemakers: for they shall be called the children of God.

St Matthew, 5:9

We try to acquire so many things of the world, but find no peace in them. The source of all happiness is within us. We have only to find out, know, and realise it.

SWAMI RAMDAS

The peace of the celestial city is the perfectly ordered and harmonious enjoyment of God and of one another in God. The peace of all things is the tranquillity of order.

ST AUGUSTINE

Rabbi Bunam taught: 'Our sages say: "Seek peace in your own place." You cannot find peace anywhere save in your own self. In the psalm we read, "There is no peace in bones because of my sin." When a man has made peace within himself, he will be able to make peace in the whole world.'

Forms of Prayer for Jewish Worship

I will endure words that hurt in silent peace as the strong elephant endures in battle arrows sent by the bow, for many people lack self-control.

They take trained elephants to battle, and kings ride on royal trained elephants. The best of men are self-trained men, those who can endure abuse in peace.

Dhammapada

All things in motion desire to make known their own proper movement, and this is an aspiration after the Divine Peace of the whole, which, unfalling, preserves all things from falling, and, unmoved, guards the idiosyncracy and life of all moving things, so that the things moved, being at peace among themselves, perform their own proper functions.

DIONYSIUS THE AREOPAGITE

The upward flight of the soul is always towards its perfect identity with the Great One who is the same through and in all. The river of life struggles through all obstacles and conditions to reach the vast and infinite ocean of existence – God. It knows no rest, no freedom and no peace until it mingles with the waters of immortality and delights in the vision of infinity.

SWAMI RAMDAS

Lead us from the individual to the Universal.

ALICE A. BAILEY

Now the city of God is called in the Hebrew Jerusalem and its name when translated is 'vision of peace'. Therefore, do not seek for the city of the Existent among the regions of the earth, since it is not wrought of wood or stone, but in a soul, in which there is no warring, whose sight is keen, which has set before it as its aim to live in contemplation and peace.

PHILO

When Peace is made between great enemies,
Some enmity is bound to remain undispelled.
How can this be considered perfect?
Therefore the sage takes the left-hand tally, but exacts no payment
    from the people.
The man of virtue takes charge of the tally;
The man of no virtue takes charge of exaction.
It is the way of heaven to show no favouritism.
It is for ever on the side of the good man.

LAO TZU

The first peace, which is the most important, is that which comes within the souls of men when they realize their relationships, their oneness, with the universe and all its Powers, and when they realize that at the center of the universe dwells *Wakan-Tanka* [the Supreme Being], and that this center is really everywhere, it is within each of us. This is the real Peace, and the others are but reflections of this. The second peace is that which is made between two individuals, and the third is that which is made between two nations. But above all you should understand that there can never be peace between nations until there is first known that true peace which, as I have often said, is within the souls of men.

BLACK ELK

Truth is the only resting-place of the soul; it is its atonement and peace with God; all is and must be disquiet, a succession of lying vanities, till the soul is again in the truth in which God at first created it. And therefore, said Truth, 'Learn of me, for I am meek and lowly of heart; and ye shall find rest unto your souls.'

WILLIAM LAW

All God wants of man is a peaceful heart; then he performs within the soul an act too Godlike for creature to attain to or yet see. The divine Wisdom is discreetly fond and lets no creature watch.

MEISTER ECKHART

Children, that peace which is found in the spirit and the inner life is well worth our care, for in that peace lies the satisfaction of all our wants. In it the Kingdom of God is discovered and His righteousness is found. This peace a man should allow nothing to take from him, whatever betide, come weal or woe, honour or shame.

JOHN TAULER

Lo! the God-fearing are among gardens and watersprings.
'Enter them in peace, secure.'
And We remove whatever burning venom may be in their breasts.
    As brethren, face to face, they rest on couches raised.
Toil cometh not unto them there, nor will they be expelled from
    thence.
Announce unto My slaves that verily I am the Forgiving, the
    Merciful.

Qur'ân, xv.45–9

All that I can offer to Jesus is the prayer that His Holy Will be accomplished. I find myself so indifferent, so foreign to everything, that I dare compare myself to a child sleeping on the Divine Heart. From the day that I abandoned myself to Him, in asking that He occupy Himself with my whole person, I have enjoyed an enviable peace and felt a constant joy.

SISTER CONSOLATA

Let the soul that is not unworthy of the vision contemplate the Great Soul; freed from deceit and every witchery and collected into calm. Calmed be the body for it in that hour and the tumult of the flesh, ay, all that is about calm; calm be the earth, the sea, the air, and let heaven itself be still. Then let it feel how into that silent heaven the Great Soul floweth in!

PLOTINUS

I am one with my group brothers, and all that I have is theirs.
May the love which is in my soul pour forth to them.
May the strength which is in me lift and aid them.
May the thoughts which my soul creates reach and encourage them.

ALICE A. BAILEY

You are in the world of things that come to be, and yet you seek to be at rest. But how can anything be at rest in the world of things that come to be? A boat, as long as it floats on the water, cannot be still or at rest; or if at any moment it is still, it is so only by chance, and forthwith the water begins again to shake and toss the things which float upon its surface. Then only is the boat at rest, when it is taken out of the water, and drawn up on the land, which is the place of the boat's origin, and is on a par with the boat in density and weight; then, but not till then, is the boat truly at rest. And even so, the soul, as long as it is involved in the processes of the physical world, cannot be still, nor be at rest, nor get any respite; but if it returns to its source and root, then it is still and is at rest, and reposes from the misery and debasement of its wandering in a foreign land.

HERMES TRISMEGISTUS

Every one thirsts for peace, but few people understand that perfect peace cannot be obtained so long as the inner soul is not filled with the presence of God . . . this God who is always present in all the fibres of your body and who none the less prefers to remain hidden. When through appropriate and assiduous exercises the blackness of your soul is effaced, God reveals Himself, and it is absolute peace.

ANANDA MOYÎ

To thee, O God, we turn for peace . . . but grant us too the blessed assurance that nothing shall deprive us of that peace, neither ourselves, nor our foolish, earthly desires, nor my wild longings, nor the anxious craving of my heart.

SØREN KIERKEGAARD

Our wills are quiescent in the nature of love; here love is fate; and in this blessed being all our wills are held in the divine will, where all are made into one will; and his will is our peace.

DANTE ALIGHIERI

Give peace, that is, continue and preserve it; give peace, that is, give us hearts worthy of it, and thankful for it. In our time, that is, all our time: for there is more besides a fair morning required to make a fair day.

THOMAS FULLER

In neither pain nor joy is liberation found.
In neither dark nor light will the spiritual sun appear.
The pairs of opposites distract the eyes of men.
Only the single eye directs the steps
Of the initiate upon the Way.

ALICE A. BAILEY

The Service of Love

We are too half-hearted in the service of Love,
And so we are not her true possession
And remain poor; but all of us should know this:
To the one of whom Love approves,
She gives her kingdom and her treasure.

HADEWIJCH OF BRABENT

I am still.
I listen and see the silence.
I listen and embrace the silence.
I enter into the great silence.
Though hidden, Grandfather dwells in all.

JOHN REDTAIL FREESOUL

CHAPTER THREE

POEMS, SONGS AND CHANTS

(In Celebration of the Dream of Peace)

All songs are a part of Him, who wears a form of sound.

Vishnu Purana

Poetry – at its best a form of magical incantation, a spinning and weaving of words in order to create a *frisson* in the mind and the soul of the reader – not infrequently deals with the subject of peace. Poets as varied and as widely separated in time and space as the anonymous ancient Egyptian author of 'The Song of the Harper' on p. 60 (found written on the walls of a tomb from the second millennium BC) and contemporary poets such as Kathleen Raine, Wendell Berry and Mary Oliver have all turned, at some point, to this theme.

So, too, have song writers, and since songs are themselves often indistinguishable from poems, some are printed here. But above all are the chants, which are both poems and songs, and which, like the seed thoughts and prayers, can stir the consciousness and open the heart and mind to the infinite different ways of achieving peace. William Anderson's 'Incantation' begins this chapter, offering advice that we should bear in mind when reading each and every poem, song or chant in this book.

In this section are shaman songs by those who have always recognised the importance of chant and the mind-changing power of rhythm. Here are mystical songs, and profane songs, and songs which look into the darker side of Creation and see hope there, even in the face of overwhelming odds.

Poems are themselves distillations of a truth, of which even the writer may be unaware. As you read in silence, or chant aloud (Yeats maintained that all poetry should be sung; David Jones counselled reading his work aloud; and Allen Ginsberg has set many of his poems to music), let your mind open itself to the possibilities expressed in this form. Consider music itself as one of the most vital paths to peace – for, as the Roman writer Quintilian said in *De musica*, 'Music . . . in remote times was not only cultivated, but venerated to such an extent that the same men were regarded as musicians, poets and sages, among whom Orpheus . . . because he tamed savage and unruly spirits by charming them . . . gained a reputation not only for moving wild beasts, but even rocks and trees.'

When we sing, or even just listen to the harmony of sound, we are in touch with the deeper reaches of the cosmos, where ultimate harmony already exists, and where the notes of celestial music may ever be heard by those who know how to listen.

Incantation

Let waves of warm words
Surge with our thoughts;
Let images like birds
Alight in our hearts;
Let rhythm's enchantment
Heal hurt and strife;
May we make of this moment
A poem in life.

WILLIAM ANDERSON

The Song of the Harper

Rejoice and let thy heart forget the day when they shall lay thee to
  rest.
Cast all sorrow behind thee, and bethink thee of joy until there
  come that day of reaching port in the land that loveth silence.
Follow thy desire as long as thou livest, put myrrh on thy head,
  clothe thee in fine linen.
Set singing and music before thy face.
Increase yet more the delights which thou hast, and let not thy heart
  grow faint. Follow thine inclination and thy profit. Do thy
  desires upon earth, and trouble not thine heart until that day
  of lamentation come to thee.
Spend a happy day and weary not thereof. Lo, none may take his
  goods with him, and none that hath gone may come again.

Ancient Egyptian

Christmas List

Dear Santa Claus,
a warship please,
a guided missile
and a bomb:
perhaps some napalm
and a set
to liquidate
the turbo jet.
I think I'll have a radar screen,
a tube of germs
that can't be seen –
and if you've still got space you might
bring a figure of Christ
to set alight.

MOYRA CALDECOTT

Psalm of the King of Beauty

From the Isles of Separation and the Empire of the Depths, hear the rising voice of the harps of the suns. Peace flows over our heads. The place where we now stand, Machut, is the heart of Height.

The fruitful tears pour forth as I think of my Father and the worlds of gold shed a light of beauty on the depths. Royal head yet resting on my heart, what a fear of numbers you decipher in the memory of night! Queen, be truly a woman in supreme compassion. All white with pity for greatness, think of the Creator, most abandoned of all. The spot where we now stand, Malchut, is the heart of Height.

Facing the saintly toil of the constellations, can you not feel your heart torn asunder, Malchut, Malchut, wife, mother too of generations? Space, a swarm of sacred bees, flies towards the Adramand of ecstatic perfumes. The spot where we now stand, Malchut, is the heart of Height.

For the motionless Absolute is the secret desire of that which moves. A solar regent and pious Sower of seed destined to be born and die, I love only what is permanent. I myself, I who am but a small personification, I desire ardently to become transmuted. Here in the abyss, nothing is situated, nothing is situated! All reality exists only in the love of the Father. The place where we now stand, Malchut, is the heart of Height.

Peace on earth, oh my spouse, oh woman! Peace in all the unreal empire, peace for the gentle souls for which you make the seven strings of the rainbow sing! When I contemplate, oh Queen, your overturned face, I have the deep feeling that all my thoughts are born in your sweet heart. The place where we now stand, Malchut, is the heart of Height.

O. V. DE L. MIŁOSZ

Misunderstanding

'Gaia, my mother,' said the Dolphin,
'all I ask is clean water in which to swim and play and praise you.
Why then am I dying in a polluted ocean? I do not understand.'

'Gaia, my mother,' said the Elephant,
'all I need is freedom to roam, sweet water and green food.
Why then am I tortured and killed by Man? I do not understand.'

'Gaia, my mother,' whispered the laboratory Rat,
'all I did was to be born in a cage filled with fear and dread.
Why am I filled with drugs, and made to die in pain? I do not
    understand.'

'Gaia, my mother,' said the Rainforest,
'I grew in strength and joy and gave food and protection to others.
Why am I now destroyed and burned? I do not understand.'

'Gaia, my mother,' said the Man,
'I have killed you and those who were my brothers and sisters in
    life.

Where did I go wrong? I do not understand.'

'Gaia, my joy and my pride,' said God,
'I created you with so much hope and filled you with My own
    Lifeforce.
Forgive Me; they did not understand.'

DOLORES ASHCROFT-NOWICKI

The Horsewomen

We stand on a high hill under heaven
watching over the wasted lands,
parched land and drowned land,
barren, burned and bombed
lands of our fathers:

And we, too, ride upon the wheel,
the black steed and the white; the pale horse and the red;
four great horses, four queens,

The white horse of healing,
the pale gold of fruitfulness,
the red horse of harmony,
the dark horse of rebirth.

We ride the wasted lands and bring healing
in the thunder of hoofbeats,
fertile, the earth, in the speed of our passing,
flaunting the pennants of our power,
red, the air in our nostrils as we drink the wind;

Springs welling from the hooves of the white mare,
flowers from the feet of the golden mare,
birds burst from the steps of the red mare,
living flame from the hooves of the black mare.

Follow the thunder of our passing
into new lives,
dark, our shadow, long on the land;
green, the earth beneath us, drumming dance of swiftness,
gold, the light within our eyes, we see the sun before us;
we are one, unstoppable, untameable, untouchable,
and are yours, are yours, in the power of love.

WOLFE VAN BRUSSEL

War God's Horse Song I

I am the Turquoise Woman's son.
On top of Belted Mountain
beautiful horses – slim like a weasel!
My horse with a hoof like a striped agate,
with his fetlock like a fine eagle plume:
my horse whose legs are like quick lightning
whose body is an eagle-plumed arrow:
my horse whose tail is like a trailing black cloud.
The Little Holy Wind blows thru his hair.
My horse with a mane made of short rainbows.
My horse with ears made of round corn.
My horse with eyes made of big stars.
My horse with a head made of mixed waters.
My horse with teeth made of white shell.
The long rainbow is in his mouth for a bridle
     & with it I guide him.
When my horse neighs, different-colored horses follow.
When my horse neighs, different-colored sheep follow.
     I am wealthy because of him.

     Before me peaceful
     Behind me peaceful
     Under me peaceful
     Over me peaceful –
     Peaceful voice when he neighs.
I am everlasting & peaceful.
I stand for my horse.

Navajo Indian: words by Tall Kia ahni;
interpreted by Louis Watchman

Song to Quiet the Ocean

Sea Spirit
Sea Spirit
calm the waves
for me
I'm tired
ye ho lo
calm the sea
for me

Come close
my spirit power
come close
to my canoe
my heart is worn
ye ho lo
turn waves
to milk
for me

Sea Spirit
Sea Spirit
calm the waves
for me
I'm tired
ye ho lo
calm the sea
for me

Traditional Haida Indian,
adapted by David Cloutier

Praying to the World

Praying to world to get better
(I can't tie a bandage around it
but I can still pray)
I invoke the idea of peace –

peace that stands by itself,
that has no supporters
save us – the stewards
of the earth,
the magic shamans
who live in the shadow
but find light . . .

Dancing on a feather
I see that the sun
has come full circle
and that the shadow
has passed.

Let's go then,
let's dance
the truth we see –
peace everywhere,
peace, peace, peace!

JOHN MATTHEWS

Peace

When will you ever, Peace, wild wooddove, shy wings shut,
Your round me roaming end, and under be my boughs?
When, when, Peace, will you, Peace? I'll not play hypocrite
To own my heart: I yield you do come sometimes; but
That piecemeal peace is poor peace. What pure peace allows
Alarms of wars, the daunting wars, the death of it?

O surely, reaving Peace, my Lord should leave in lieu
Some good! And so he does leave Patience exquisite,
That plumes to Peace thereafter. And when Peace here does house
He comes with work to do, he does not come to coo,
        He comes to brood and sit.

GERARD MANLEY HOPKINS

Autumnal

Why in mind's eye
My mother's mother, smiling
Among the gold-veined vine-leaves,
Sun-caressed, in bliss
Of age, earth's grandmother-face?
I never saw her goddess-form until today
Who is loam, is forgotten, yet lives on
In generation, in memories and visions
Of the one unending azure sky.

KATHLEEN RAINE

Yucatec-Maya Song

You are singing, little dove,
on the branches of the silk-cotton tree.
And there also is the cuckoo,
and many other little birds.
All are rejoicing,
the songbirds of our god, our Lord.
And our goddess
has her little birds,
the turtledove, the redbird,
the black and yellow songbirds, and the hummingbird.
These are the birds of the beautiful goddess, our Lady.
If there is such happiness
among the creatures,
why do our hearts not also rejoice?
At daybreak all is jubliant.
Let only joy, only songs,
enter our thoughts!

Only Thee
do I trust entirely,
here where one dwells.
For thou, O great Kin,
providest that which is good,
here where one dwells,
to all living beings.
Since Thou abidest to give reality to the earth,
where all men live.
And Thou are the true helper
who grants that which is good . . .

Traditional Mexoamerican,
trans. Miguel Léon-Portilla

The Rain Cloud

It is like a great cloud rising above the world,
Covering all things everywhere –
A gracious cloud full of moisture; lightning-flames flash and dazzle,
Voice of thunder vibrates afar, bringing joy and ease to all.
The sun's rays are veiled, and the earth is cooled;
The cloud lowers and spreads as if it might be caught and gathered;
Its rain everywhere equally descends on all sides,
Streaming and pouring unstinted, permeating the land.
On mountains, by rivers, in valleys,
In hidden recesses, there grow the plants, trees, and herbs;
Trees, both great and small, the shoots of the ripening grain,
Grape vine and sugar cane.
Fertilized are these by the rain and abundantly enriched;
The dry ground is soaked; herbs and trees flourish together.
From the one water which is issued from that cloud,
Plants, trees, thickets, forests, according to need receive moisture.
All the various trees, lofty, medium, low, each according to its size,
Grows and develops roots, stalks, branches, leaves,
Blossoms and fruits in their brilliant colors;
Wherever the one rain reaches, all become fresh and glossy.
According as their bodies, forms, and natures are great and small,
So the enriching rain, though it is one and the same,
Yet makes each of them flourish.
In like manner also the Buddha appears here in the world
Like unto a great cloud universally covering all things;
And having appeared in the world, for the sake of living,
He discriminates and proclaims the truth in regard to all laws.
The Great Holy World – honored One among the gods and
     humans,
And among all living beings proclaims abroad this word:
'I am the Tathagata, the Most Honored among humans;
I appear in the world like this great cloud,
To pour enrichment on all parched living beings,
To free them from their misery to attain the joy of peace,
Joy of the present world and joy of Nirvana . . .
Everywhere impartially, without distinction of persons . . .
Ever to all beings I preach the Law equally; . . .
Equally I rain the Law – rain untiringly.'

From the *Lotus Sutra*

Resurrection

Sweet Peace, where dost thou dwell? I humbly crave
 Let me once know.
 I sought thee in a secret cave,
  And ask'd if Peace were there.
A hollow wind did seem to answer, 'No;
 Go seek elsewhere.'

I did; and going did a rainbow note:
 Surely, thought I,
 This is the lace of Peace's coat:
  I will search out the matter.
But while I look'd, the clouds immediately
 Did break and scatter.

Then went I to a garden, and did spy
 A gallant flower,
 The Crown Imperial. Sure, said I
  Peace at the root must dwell.
But when I digg'd, I saw a worm devour
 What show'd so well.

At length I met a rev'rend good old man,
 Whom when for Peace
 I did demand, he thus began:
  'There was a Prince of old
At Salem dwelt, Who liv'd with good increase
 Of flock and fold.

'He sweetly liv'd; yet sweetness did not save
   His life from foes.
But after death out of His grave
   There sprang twelve staks of wheat;
Which many wond'ring at, got some of those
   To plant and set.

'It prosper'd strangely, and did soon disperse
   Through all the earth;
For they that taste it do rehearse
   That virtue lies therein;
A secret virtue, bringing peace and mirth
   By flight of sin.

'Take of this grain, which in my garden grows
   And grows for you;
Make bread of it; and that repose
   And peace, which ev'ry where
With so much earnestness you do pursue,
   Is only there.'

GEORGE HERBERT

Into the Peace of Sophia

She runs sunwise round the circuit,
sun-wheel widening
the tight cosmology.
  We had shrunken the sun,
  netted the moon,
  counted the illimitable stars
  and charted their motions.
Now she sets the cycle turning,
Now she sets the spirit burning,
Now she sets the heart a-yearning
For a brighter day.

And the white people came
and the black people came
and the rainbow people came
and the hidden people who have no colour
because they live under stones
and could neither see or be seen –
came and saw and were astounded . . .
'But this is what we always wanted
and dreamed about,' they said.
'But we were never worthy,
we weren't pure enough
or holy enough
or rich enough
or poor enough
to join the sun-circle
and the singing.'

And Sophia laughed and clapped her hands:
'Well now, you can all join my dance
and run the sun-wise circle.'
And they said they couldn't dance
because they'd never had lessons,
and they said they couldn't run
because their legs weren't fast enough,
and some asked if they couldn't run
in the opposite direction and why.

And as they argued and made excuses
for their deplorable inability,
the sun slipped sideways
under the horizon
and darkness fell.

She runs moonwise the circuit,
moon-wheel widening
the tight cosmology.
  We had shrunken the sun,
  netted the moon,
  counted the illimitable stars
  and charted their motions.
Now she sets the phases spinning,
now she hastens the beginning
of a dance that will be winning
us a shining night.

And the black people
began a singing and dancing
that sounded horribly tribal.
And the white people
complained about the noise
and the insistent rhythm.
And the rainbow people ignored them
and joined in.
And the hidden people
from under the stones
stood indecisively on the fringes
and said nothing,
though their eyes gleamed
like glow-worms in the moonlight.

And Sophia laughed and clapped her hands:
'Well now, you can all join my dance
and run the moon-wise circle.'
And some questioned the wisdom of this
because the moon was a changeable goddess,
and some were unhappy
because the moon was in the wrong phase.

And as they debated the question
of whether God was a man or a woman,
the moon slipped sideways
like a saucer
over the rim of the world
and there was darkness.

She runs star-wise the circuit,
star-wheel widening
the tight cosmology.
    We had shrunken the sun,
    netted the moon,
        counted the illimitable stars
        and charted their motions.
Now she sends the planets gliding,
sends the meteor-showers sliding,
brings them all to her abiding
and her transient home.

And the white people sat up
and admired the fireworks
and didn't mind it
when the black and rainbow people
shouted 'Ooh' and 'Ah' with them.
And the hidden people
from under the stones
were beginning to see her light.
And when the stars began singing
they all sang too
the old song of the stairway to bed.

And she led them
into the spiral dance
of the Milky Way.
And every one of them
knew the steps
and everyone of them
knew the words of the song.
And the sevenfold stair
wound up to bed.

And no one said that they weren't tired yet,
and no on said that they hadn't played long enough,
and no one said that they wanted another story,
for she told them a new story
every night of the cosmic week.
And when she had finished folding their clothes away,
she began to think of a new dance to lead them in
when the clock of the dawning age struck seven.

CAITLÍN MATTHEWS

Sequence for the Holy Spirit

Fiery Spirit,
fount of courage
life within life
of all that has being!

Holy are you, transmuting the perfect
     into the real.
Holy are you, healing
     the mortally stricken.
Holy are you, cleansing
     the stench of wounds.

O sacred breath O blazing
love O savor in the breast and balm
flooding the heart with
the fragrance of good,

O limpid mirror of God
who leads wanderers
home and hunts out the lost,

Armor of the heart and hope
of the integral body,
sword-belt of honor:
save those who know bliss!

Guard those the fiend holds
imprisoned,
free those in fetters
whom divine force wishes to save.

O current of power permeating all
in the heights upon the earth and
in all deeps:
you bind and gather
all people together.

ST HILDEGARD OF BINGEN

Responsory for the Holy Innocents

Our king is swift to receive
the blood of innocents:
angels in concert chime their praise.

But for blood that was spilled
the clouds are grieving.

In a grave dream the tyrant
was choked for his malice.

But for blood that was spilled
the clouds are grieving.

Glorify the Father,
the Spirit and the Son.

But for blood that was spilled
the clouds are grieving.

ST HILDEGARD OF BINGEN

Suddenly
It was as if I had been,
This life-time no longer mine

To bear, and freed by loss
Boundless.

Then who was? No one!
Who free? Not I!

That bliss
Music's transience as the air
Trembles.

KATHLEEN RAINE

Peace

I seek for peace – I care not where 'tis found:
  On this rude scene in briers and brambles drest,
If peace dwells here, 'tis consecrated ground,
  And owns the power to give my bosom rest;
To soothe the rankling of each bitter wound,
  Gall'd by rude envy's adder-biting jest,
And worldly strife – ah, I am looking round
for peace's hermitage, can it be found? –
Surely that breeze that o'er the blue wave curl'd
Did whisper soft, 'Thy wanderings here are blest.'
How different from the language of the world!
Nor jeers nor taunts in this still spot are given:
Its calm's a balsam to a soul distrest;
And, where peace smiles, a wilderness is heaven.

JOHN CLARE

Poem for Peace

Black-headed Gulls on the Thames

The hooded nuns hasten along the corridors,
Frantic the day's hours and the search for God.
Flags echo wars, and like the pain of peace
That cannot come this way, the gulls veer
Away over mountains of sea, dividing us.
Like nuns the gulls are hooded in my heart.

In winter the harsh cry of the wandering ones
Harries the earth's worms. Where is your hood
In winter, wandering gull, I wonder where?
Or when at summer's close you cast it off,
Gull, did you know that winter's war was near?
Hooded gull, my summer gull, put off your hood!

PETER RUSSELL

After Hearing a Tape-recording of Music by Mechtilde of Magdeburg

I heard soul singing
In rapturous lonely voice.
Her face only god sees,

Hidden
In the heart of the one
Beloved, as in the evening

A bird alone.
Her song in praise
Of the unknown.

KATHLEEN RAINE

Anach

There is no peace now however things go,
  No peace where the ways of men ring loud,
Save in a secret place that I know
  Hidden as in a cloud.

All the high hills stand clustering round,
  Arched to protect it from trouble and noise,
The great strong hills that sing without sound,
  And speak with no voice.

There lies Caorog, the mute low lake,
  And Bun-na-freamha lying aloft,
Peacefully sleeping, or even if they wake,
  Lapping low and soft.

Upon the high hill-tops the heather may be crying,
  And over the hill-tops the voices of men are heard,
But here only water lapping and sighing,
  Or the wail of a bird.

Peace, peace and peace, from the inner heart of dream,
  More full of wisdom than speech can tell,
Dopt like a veil round the show of things that seem
  With an invisible spell.

DARRELL FIGGIS

The Divine Image

To Mercy, Pity, Peace and Love
All pray in their distress:
And to these virtues of delight
Return their thankfulness.

For Mercy, Pity, Peace and Love
Is God, our Father dear,
And Mercy, Pity, Peace and Love
Is Man, His child and care.

For Mercy has a human heart,
Pity a human face,
And Love, the human form divine,
And Peace, the human dress.

Then every man, of every clime,
That prays in his distress,
Prays to the human form divine,
Love, Mercy, Pity, Peace.

And all must love the human form,
In heathen, Turk, or Jew;
Where Mercy, Love and Pity dwell,
There God is dwelling too.

WILLIAM BLAKE

The Inner Essence of Peace

If
The inner essence
Of peace
Is
Causeless
Timeless
And therefore
Beyond words,
Then what are we doing
Writing about it?

Our words are strung out on a line
And all we see is our own washing.

JOHN-FRANCIS PHIPPS

The Guru and the Politician

'This is the only way to peace,'
    said the guru
    (who was also a bit of a politician).
So there was a war.

'This is the only way to peace,'
    said the politician
    (who was also a bit of a guru).
So there was a war.

'There is no path to peace,'
    said the anti-guru guru.
So his anti-follower followers argued among themselves
    (and so had their own cosy little war).

JOHN-FRANCIS PHIPPS

The Song of the Five Sisters

You are my sister, your skin black as night.
A princess of the Royal blood in the arms of Solomon the King.
Your beauty is different to mine but love is common to us both.
Yours is Saba, the Land of the South, rich in gold and spices,
   where the sun's heat soaks into the parched earth.
Yes, you are my sister and together we shall live in peace.

You are my sister, with a body the colour of fine gold.
Your eyes follow the gentle curve of the almond, dark and
   mysterious.
In your veins flows the blood of the Seven Immortals, old as time
   itself.
The Dragon Throne was yours in that time and still awaits your
   return.
Cherry blossom floating on a still pool where golden fishes play.
Yes, you are my sister and together we shall live in peace.

You are my sister, your breasts are the colour of warm earth.
Soft as the voice of Rama, strong as the sword of Kali is your soul.
Generations of proud men, Kings and Warriors have sought your
   love.
The snow-capped mountains of the north have taught you
   endurance.
In the Art of Love you are without equal, daughter of Brahma.
Yes, you are my sister and together we shall live in peace.

You are my sister, your arms show the bronze of many Tribes.
In you hair shines the wing of the raven braided with quills and
   wampum.
Under your skilled fingers a weaver's loom gives birth to beauty
   and colour.
Silver and turquoise are your marriage gifts, proud is your race and
   heritage.
Bitter have been your tears, and sorrow has been your companion.
Yes, you are my sister and together we shall live in peace.

Listen to my song, O my sisters, my face is white, pale as the moon.
Like you I live and love, bear children, grow old and will die,
yet I sing my song of hope for those that will follow us along the
Path,
Throughout the Western Lands I sing the Song of Peace of Peace
between us.
Black and white, red and gold and brown, we are the women, the
mothers.
Yes, you are my sisters, and together we shall live in peace.

DOLORES ASHCROFT-NOWICKI

Our Planet's Dream

We hold our planet's death
as lightly as a smiling child
holds an unpinned hand grenade.

MOYRA CALDECOTT

The Peace of Wild Things

When despair for the world grows in me
and I wake in the night at the least sound
in fear of what my life and my children's lives may be,
I go and lie down where the wood drake
rests in his beauty on the water, and the great heron feeds.
I come into the peace of wild things
who do not tax their lives with forethought
of grief. I come into the presence of still water.
And I feel above me the day-blind stars
waiting with their light. For a time
I rest in the grace of the world, and am free.

WENDELL BERRY

Sleeping in the Forest

I thought the earth
remembered me, she
took me back so tenderly, arranging
her dark skirts, her pockets
full of lichens and seeds. I slept
as never before, a stone
on the riverbed, nothing
between me and the white fire of the stars
but my thoughts, and they floated
light as moths among the branches
of the perfect trees. All night
I heard the small kingdoms breathing
around me, the insects, and the birds
who do their work in the darkness. All night
I rose and fell, as if in water, grappling
with a luminous doom. By morning
I had vanished at least a dozen times
into something better.

MARY OLIVER

Stone

Go inside a stone.
That would be my way.
Let somebody else become a dove
Or gnash with a tiger's tooth.
I am happy to be a stone.

From the outside the stone is a riddle:
No one knows how to answer it.
Yet within, it must be cool and quiet
Even though a cow steps on it full weight,
Even though a child throws it in a river;
The stone sinks, slow, unperturbed
To the river bottom
Where the fishes come to knock on it
And Listen.

I have seen sparks fly out
When two stones are rubbed,
So perhaps it is not dark inside after all;
Perhaps there is a moon shining
From somewhere, as though behind a hill –
Just enough light to make out
The strange writings, the star-charts
On the inner walls.

CHARLES SIMIC

The Prisoner

But first a hush of peace, a soundless calm descends;
The struggle of distress and fierce impatience ends;
Mute music soothes my breast; unuttered harmony
That I could never dream till earth was lost to me.

Then dawns the Invisible, the Unseen its truth reveals;
My outward sense is gone, my inward essence feels
Its wings are almost free, its home, its harbour found;
Measuring the gulf it stoops and dares the final bound!

Oh dreadful is the check, intense the agony,
When the ear begins to hear and the eye begins to see;
When the pulse begins to throb, the brain to think again,
The soul to feel the flesh and the flesh to feel the chain!

Yet I would lose no sting, would wish no torture less;
The more the anguish racks the earlier it will bless;
And robed in fires of hell, or bright with heavenly shine,
If it but herald death, the vision is divine!

EMILY BRONTË

Peace

I sought for Peace, but could not find;
   I sought it in the city,
But they were of another mind,
   The more's the pity!

I sought for Peace of country swain,
   But yet I could not find;
So I, returning home again,
   Left Peace behind.

Sweet Peace, where dost thou dwell? said I.
   Methought a voice was given:
'Peace dwelt not here, long since did fly
   To God in heaven.'

Thought I, this echo is but vain,
   To folly 'tis of kin;
Anon I heard it tell me plain,
   'Twas killed by sin.

Then I believed the former voice,
   And rested well content,
Laid down and slept, rose, did rejoice,
   And then to heaven went.
There I enquired for peace, and found it true,
An heavenly plant it was, and sweetly grew.

SAMUEL SPEED

Sunset

Fold upon fold of light,
Half-heaven of tender fire,
Conflagration of peace,
Wide hearth of the evening world.
How can a cloud give peace,
Peace speaks through bodiless fire
And still the angry world?

Yet now each bush and tree
Stands still within the fire,
And the bird sits on the tree.
Three horses in a field
That yesterday ran wild
Are bridled and reigned by light
As in a heavenly field.
Man, beast and tree in fire,
The bright cloud showering peace.

EDWIN MUIR

Love is Not Something You Do

Love is not something you do,
It is not how you behave.
There's nothing you can do that constitutes loving another,
No action that is of itself loving.
Love is a way of being.
And more than that.
It is simply being,
Being with another person, however they may be.
Holding no judgements, having no agendas,
No need to have them experience your love,
No desire to demonstrate love,
No intrusion upon their soul.
Nothing but a total acceptance of their being,
Born of your total acceptance of yours.

PETER RUSSELL

For the Children

The rising hills, the slopes
of statistics
lie before us,
the steep climb
of everything, going up,
up, as we all
go down.

In the next century
or the one beyond that, they say,
are valleys, pastures,
we can meet there in peace
if we make it.

To climb these coming crests
one word to you, to
you and your children:

stay together
learn the flowers
go light.

GARY SNYDER

Shanti Path

ASATO MĀ SAD GAMAYĀ
TAMASO MĀ JYOTIR GAMAYĀ
MRITYOR MĀ AMRITAM GAMAYĀ

SARVESHAM SVASTIR BHAVATU
SARVESHAM SHANTIR BHAVATU
SARVESHAM POORNAM BHAVATU
SARVESHAM MANGALAM BHAVATU

LOKĀ SAMASTĀ SUKHINO BHAVANTU

OM TRAYAM BAKAM YAJAMAHE
SUGANDHIM PUSHTI VARDHANAM
URVĀ RUKAMIVĀ BANDHANAT
MRITYOR MUKSHIYA MAM RITAT

OM SHANTI SHANTI SHANTI.

From the unreal lead me to the real
From darkness lead me to light
From death lead me to immortality

May all beings dwell in happiness
May all beings dwell in peace
May all beings attain oneness
May all beings attain auspiciousness

May happiness be unto the whole world

We worship the three-eyed one (Shiva), who is fragrant and who nourishes all beings. May he liberate all beings. May he liberate us from death for the sake of immortality, even as the cucumber is severed from the vine.

Peace, Peace, Peace.

Psalm of Reintegration

In the middle of the night, I sometimes happen to be awakened by the most perfect silence of the whole universe. It is then as if suddenly the celestial hosts, perceiving in my thought the assigned goal of their course, stopped dead above my head in order to consider me while holding their breath. As in the distant days of my childhood, all my soul reaches out towards the great voice which is preparing to summon me from the depths of created spaces. But I wait in vain, and the peace that surrounds me is so perfect only because it no longer has a name to bestow on me. It is in me and I am in it, and in that Place that is unnamed as we are too and where our union has occurred, even the most universal word, HERE, has lost its meaning for all time, since nothing has subsisted beyond us where we might still place a THERE, and the whole space in which thought breathes appears to us to be no longer something that contains, but the illuminated interior of the Cosmos, a beautiful crystal fallen out of the hands of God. Formerly, when the spirit of perfect silence seized me, I used to raise my eyes towards the suns. Today, together with their gaze, my sight goes down into my own being, for their secret is there and not within their own selves. The place where they contemplate me is the very one where I stand, and I recognize the sorrow of my own conscience in the loving reporach that is depicted on the face of the universe. The immensity engendered by the infinity of circumscribed movements cannot possibly fill the void of my soul: there exists no height that would be accessible to the extension of the Number, the moments of which are not counted by my heartbeats. This distance between Nothing and Nothing, why should I worry about it? True, I fell from a great height, but *another kind of space* measured my fall in which the whole world fell with me. The real place, the only place that is, is in me, and that is why the Universe, my conscience, watches, awakened this night, and watches me. Oh, my Father, the name of my ill is not ignorance but forgetfulness. Lead your child back to the sources of Memory. Tell your child to return, following upstream the course of his own blood. The movement of my fall created time and space, those waters which closed above me in Space that has neither motion nor limits and for which it is beyond my powers to imagine a container. Let my ascension project the Other Space, the true, original and sanctified Space, and let the Universe that is here, the Son of my Pain, whose nocturnal gaze rests on my soul, rise together with me towards the Fatherland, in the joyful stream of babbling influences of golden beatitude.

O. V. DE L. MIŁOSZ

Peace and Rest

Under this tree, where light and shade
  Speckle the grass like a Thrush's breast,
Here, in this green and quiet place,
  I give myself to peace and rest.

The peace of my contended mind,
  That is to me a wealth untold –
When the Moon has no more silver left,
  And the Sun's at the end of his gold.

W. H. DAVIES

It is our quiet time.
We do not speak, because the voices are within us.
It is our quiet time.
We do not walk, because the earth is all within us.
It is our quiet time.
We do not dance, because the music has lifted us to a place where
    the spirit is.
It is our quiet time.
We rest with all of nature. We wake when the seven sisters wake.
We greet them in the sky over the opening of the kiva.

NANCY WOOD

Sing of a Blessing

Sing, we sing of a blessing.
Sing, we sing of a blessing.
A blessing of love. A blessing of mercy.
Love will increase a blessing of peace.

Pray now, pray for a blessing.
Pray now, pray for a blessing.
A blessing of joy. A blessing of justice.
Love will increase a blessing of peace.

Share now, share in a blessing.
Share now, share in a blessing.
A blessing of hope. A blessing of courage.
Love will increase a blessing of peace.

*Live, live, live as a blessing.
Live, live, live as a blessing.
A blessing within. A blessing among us.
Love will increase a blessing of peace.

**Rise up, rise for a blessing.
Rise up, rise for a blessing.
A blessing be yours now and forever.
Love will increase a blessing of peace.
Love will increase a blessing of peace.

(*Alternate Final Verse*)
Send forth, send forth a blessing.
Send forth, send forth a blessing.
A blessing to all now and forever.
Love will increase a blessing of peace.
Love will increase a blessing of peace.

MIRIAM THERESE WINTER

*Transpose Verse 4 up one half-tone (D Flat Major).
**Transpose Verse 5 up an additional half-tone (D Major).

Let Us Enjoy Ourselves Here and Now

For only here on earth
shall the fragrant flowers last
and the songs that are our bliss.
Enjoy them now!

One day we must go,
one night we will descend into the region of mystery.
Here, we only come to know ourselves;
only in passing are we here on earth.
In peace and pleasure let us spend our lives; come, let us enjoy
    ourselves.

Let us have friends here!
It is the time to know our faces.
Only with flowers
can our song enrapture.
We will have gone to His house,
but our word
shall live here on earth.
We will go, leaving behind
our grief, our song.
For this will be known,
the song shall remain real.
We will have gone to His house,
but our word
shall live here on earth.

I weep, I feel forlorn;
I remember that we must leave flowers and songs.
Let us enjoy ourselves now, let us sing now!
For we go, we disappear.

Remove trouble from your hearts, O my friends.
As I know, so do others:
Only once do we live.
Let us in peace and pleasure spend our lives;
come, let us enjoy ourselves!
Let not those who live in anger join us,
the earth is so vast.
Oh! that one could live forever!
Oh! that one never had to die!

Traditional Mesoamerican song,
trans. Miguel Léon-Portilla

Chant of Peace

Peace and growth to him,
Hu hi! ho ho!

Strength and worth to him,
Hu hi! ho ho!

Victory of place,
Hu hi! ho ho!

Everywhere to him,
Hu hi! ho ho!
Hu hi! hi ho!

The Mary Mother,
Hu hi! ho ho!

Fair white lovely,
Hu hi! ho ho!

Be fondling thee,
Hu hi! ho ho!

Be dandling thee,
Hu hi! ho ho!

Be bathing thee,
Hu hi! ho ho!

Be rearing thee,
Hu hi! ho ho!

Be shielding thee,
Hu hi! ho ho!

From the net of thine enemy;
Hu hi! ho ho!
Hu hi! hi ho!

Be caressing thee,
Hu hi! ho ho!

Be guarding thee,
Hu hi! ho ho!

Be filling thee,
Hu hi! ho ho!

With the graces;
Hu hi! ho ho!
Hu hi! hi ho!

The love of thy mother, thou,
Hu hi! ho ho!

The love of her love, thou,
Hu hi! ho ho!

The love of the angels, thou,
Hu hi! ho ho!

In Paradise!
Hu hi! ho ho!
Hu hi! hi ho!

Traditional Gaelic

The Return

Let there be peace between us, said the Jew, taking the hand of the
Arab.
From the thigh of Abraham we both emerged; let there be an end
of hate.

I am weary of the Sword, said the Arab, offering bread and salt to
the Jew.
Let us water our gardens from the Jordan and feed our children
together.

I need to know you as a brother, said the Tamil to the Parsee,
offering grain.
My fields hold a fine harvest; if you are hungry, share my bread.

I name you the son of my father, said the Parsee to the Tamil in
return.
Never shall your family lack shelter in the season of the monsoon.

Let me mend your broken plough, said the Hindu to the Muslim
farmer.
While I work, you shall use my plough and my oxen in your fields.

A blessing on your family, said the Muslim farmer to the Hindu.
In return I and my sons will help you harvest your crops.

Forgive me for past injustices to you, said the White man to the
Red.
Let me honour your ways, smoke your pipe and walk in your
moccasins.

Come into my Hogan, sit and eat with me, said the Red man to
the White.
Let us fill the Peace Pipe and make plans for the future of the land.

Let me bind your wounds for you, said the Black man to the
Yellow.
I have doctors and medicine for you and your children.

For this help, I will teach you ancient secrets, said the Yellow man.
Together we will strive to learn the secrets of the eternal Dao.

Lord God, now I understand why You created Humanity, said
    Lucifer.
Father, forgive me; may I return home?

You never left, said God.

DOLORES ASHCROFT-NOWICKI

Who are the Peacemakers?

Who are the peacemakers?
So many are they – the people of goodwill
Who act with compassion
And vision the oneness of life,
Whose hearts are open to the plight of others,
Who respond with wisdom to their needs.

And the paths to peace, where are they?
Wherever true service marks the way,
So easy to find, so hard to travel.

And when will peace come?
When real needs are met, only then.
For justice and trust set the pace
Of the human journey to peace,
Justice, trust and the spirit of unity,
These goals of the peacemakers
For peace through goodwill.

JAN NATION

Blessing Song

May the blessing of God go before you.
May Her grace and peace abound.
May Her Spirit live within you.
May Her love wrap you 'round.
May Her blessing remain with you always.
May you walk on holy ground.

MIRIAM THERESE WINTER

CHAPTER FOUR

CEREMONIES
(Externalising Innermost Desires)

If one only understood the meaning of these [ceremonies] ... to Heaven and Earth, and the significance of services in ancestral worship in summer and autumn, it would be as easy to give peace and order to a nation as to a point a finger at the palm.

CONFUCIUS

It is not enough, ultimately, simply to dream of peace. The question which rises again and again to trouble the minds of those who seek peace is 'What can I actually do?'. There are as many answers to this question as there are people to ask it, and none may be more valid than another. One answer is to externalise the dream in such a way that it is seen to take on a concrete form. A powerful and effective method for achieving this, for both summoning and celebrating the desired object, is the performance of ceremonies.

The ceremonies which follow were all, save four, written especially for this book. Each of them is by a respected spiritual practitioner who has taken prayer, meditation and song to a higher level – that of the ritualisation of ideas. Ritual has always been a means of contacting other levels of creation, and of externalising the inner hopes, dreams and desires of the human psyche. Employed with equal success by psychologists, anthropologists, neo-shamans, priests and priestesses of many religious affiliations, it can also be used by ordinary people without danger or compromise. Indeed such people become part of a line of transmission which stretches back to the dawn of human awareness, and which will continue until time itself is rolled up.

Ritual is a ship that carries its participants into different waters. In the words of St Gregory of Sinai: 'A ship has no need of oars when the wind swells the sails, for then the wind gives it sufficient power easily to navigate the salt sea of passions. But when the wind dies and the ship stops, it has to be set in motion by oars or by a towboat.'

Ritual provides the oars to set our craft in motion, to carry us far along the path we have chosen. Whatever the nature of our separation from a state of peace, ritual can help us find our way back. And in the times through which we have yet to live – when, beyond doubt, new threats will surround us – it is a means of focussing and concentrating our hopes for a better future. It is also, just as surely, a way of telling the lords of form and destiny that we are here, and that we have not forgotten our way.

The authors of the ceremonies that follow include (among others) a Buddhist, a Christian, a Native American wisdom-speaker, a poet, a mystic, a musician and a midwife. Each ceremony is a practical actualisation of peace in all its manifestations, easily performed by the individual or by a small group of like-minded people. Some pieces offer no more than brief instructions, or symbols upon which to meditate in active participation with the spirit of peace. All of them, if followed carefully, can help bring about the changes every one of us, each in our own way, hopes for. The words of the Native American wisdom-speaker Black Elk, which open this section, express this as well or better than anything that I could add; let us take them to heart as we prepare to celebrate the peace that we all desire.

Through these rites [the Lakota Ceremony, the Making of Relatives] a threefold peace was established. The first peace, which is the most important, is that which comes within the souls of men when they realize their relationship, their oneness, with the universe and all its Powers, and when they realize that at the center of the universe dwells *Wakan-Tanka* [the Supreme Being], and that this center is really everywhere, it is within each of us. This is our real peace, and the others are but reflections of this. The second peace is that which is made between two individuals, and the third is that which is made between two nations. But above all you should understand that there can never be peace between nations until there is first known that true peace which, as I have often said, is within the souls of men.

BLACK ELK

A Prayer for Peace

When I am facing a particular issue or situation, I find it helpful to create a ritual specifically for the matter at hand. Here is a ritual that I have created for peace.

I create a circle around myself and place a candle in front of me. From each of the cardinal directions I summon a particular force or quality.

From behind me I call the forces of our history, the forces of karma and habit active in the war, in the world, and in my own life. I greet these forces with mindfulness and offer my heart as a place for habit to be transformed into liberation and wisdom.

From in front of me I call the forces of our future and ask for the spirit of our possibilities to be present in this crisis. I ask that we do not depend on suffering to be the path into our future, but that we learn other paths based on joy, on discovery, on liberation and blessing. I ask that I may be a channel through which the potentials of a new world may find expression.

From my left I summon the forces of the Earth – the spirits of the creatures and plants, ecologies and landscapes – and ask for their assistance and protection. I ask their spirits to teach me how to live as a blessing upon the Earth. I ask for their forgiveness for the destruction we cause to the Earth and to the creatures upon it, including ourselves. I ask for their spirit to flow through our human arrogance to teach us how to embody the energies of both creation and destruction, formation and transformation.

From my right I summon the spirit of humanity. I open my heart unconditionally to embrace it in its pain and its possibility, its sorrow and its joy. I ask that I may be an agent for humanity's liberation and growth.

I bring together my right and left hands to symbolize the energy between humanity and nature. I open my heart to past and future to be a place where they can meet in mutual empowerment.

Then, from above and below, I invite the presence of the sacred to give wholeness and blessing to us all – past and future, Earth and humans. I pray for the peace that transforms us and takes us to a new world.

With this prayer, I blow out my candle and close my circle with gratefulness. As I go about my life, in the midst of images of death and destruction, I know I must also be mindful of all of the ways that life is emerging upon the Earth. It is by enhancing life in my world and in the hearts of others that I can find the grace that will heal the terrors of war and take us beyond into a new world.

DAVID SPANGLER

The Sevenfold Peace
(To be read aloud in company)

Peace I bring to thee, my children,
The Sevenfold Peace
Of the Earthly Mother
and the Heavenly Father.
Peace I bring to they body,
Guided by the Angel of Power;
Peace I bring to thy heart,
Guided by the Angel of Love;
Peace I bring to thy mind,
Guided by the Angel of Wisdom.
Through the Angels of
Power, Love and Wisdom,
Thou shalt travel the Seven Paths
Of the Infinite Garden,
And thy body, thy heart and thy mind
Shall join in Oneness
In the Sacred Flight to the
Heavenly Sea of Peace.

Yea, I tell thee truly,
The paths are seven
Through the Infinite Garden,
And each must be traversed
By the body, the heart and the mind
As one,
Lest thou stumble and fall
Into the abyss of emptiness.
For as a bird cannot fly with one wing,
So doth thy Bird of Wisdom
Need two wings of Power and Love
To soar above the abyss
To the Holy Tree of Life.

For the body alone
Is an abandoned house seen from afar:
What was thought beautiful
Is but ruin and desolation
When drawing near.
The body alone

Is as a chariot fashioned from gold,
Whose maker sets it on a pedestal,
Loath to soil it with use.
But as a golden idol,
It is ugly and without grace,
For only in movement
Doth it reveal its purpose.
Like the hollow blackness of a window
When the wind puts out its candle,
Is the body alone,
With no heart and no mind
To fill it with light.

And the heart alone
Is a sun with no earth to shine upon,
A light in the void,
A ball of warmth drowned
In a sea of blackness.
For when a man doth love,
That love turneth only to
Its own destruction
When there is no hand to stretch forth
In good works,
And no mind to weave the flames of desire
Into a trapestry of psalms.
Like a whirlwind in the desert
Is the heart alone,
With no body and no mind
To lead it singing
Through the cypress and the pine.

And the mind alone
Is a holy scroll
Which was worn thin with the years,
And must be buried.
The truth and beauty of its words
Have not changed,
But the eyes can no longer read
The faded letters,
And it falleth to pieces in the hands.
So is the mind without heart
To give it words,
And without the body

To do its deeds.
For what availeth wisdom
Without a heart to feel
And a tongue to give it voice?
Barren as the womb of an aged woman
Is the mind alone,
With no heart and no body
To fill it with life.

For, lo, I tell thee truly,
The body and the heart and the mind
Are as a chariot, and a horse, and a driver.
The chariot is the body,
Forged in strength to do the will
Of the Heavenly Father
And the Earthly Mother.
The heart is the fiery steed,
Glorious and courageous,
Who carries the chariot bravely,
Whether the road be smooth,
Or whether stones and fallen trees
Lie in its path.
And the driver is the mind,
Holding the reins of wisdom,
Seeing from above what lieth
On the far horizon,
Charting the course of hoofs and wheels.

Give ear, O ye heavens,
And I will speak;
And hear, O earth,
The words of my mouth.
My doctrine shall drop as the rain,
My speech shall distill as the dew,
As the small rain
Upon the tender herb,
And as the showers upon the grass.

Blessed is the Child of Light
Who is strong in body,
For he shall have oneness with the earth.
Thou shalt celebrate a daily feast
With all the gifts of the Angel of Earth:

The golden wheat and corn,
The purple grapes of autumn,
The ripe fruits of the trees,
The amber honey of the bees.
Thou shalt seek the fresh air
Of the forest and of the fields,
And there in the midst of them
Shalt thou find the Angel of Air.
Put off thy shoes and clothing
And suffer the Angel of Air
To embrace all thy body.
Then shalt thou breathe long and deeply,
That the Angel of Air
May be brought within thee.
Enter into the cool and flowing river
And suffer the Angel of Water
To embrace all thy body.
Cast thyself wholly into his enfolding arms,
And as often as thou movest the air
With thy breath,
Move with thy body the water also.
Thou shalt seek the Angel of Sun,
And enter into that embrace
Which doth purify with holy flames.
And all these things are of the Holy Law
Of the Earthly Mother,
She who did give thee birth.
He who hath found peace with the body
Hath built a holy temple
Wherein may dwell forever
The spirit of God.
Know this peace with thy mind,
Desire this peace with thy heart,
Fulfill this peace with thy body.

Blessed is the Child of Light
Who is wise in mind,
For he shall create heaven.
The mind of the wise
Is a well-plowed field,
Which giveth forth abundance and plenty.
For it thou showest a handful of seed

To a wise man,
He will see in his mind's eye
A field of golden wheat.
And if thou showest a handful of seed
To a fool,
He will see only that which is before him,
And call them worthless pebbles.
And as the field of the wise man
Giveth forth grain in abundance,
And the field of the fool
Is a harvest only of stones,
So it is with our thoughts.
As the sheaf of golden wheat
Lieth hidden within the tiny kernel,
So is the kingdom of heaven
Hidden within our thoughts.
If they be filled with the
Power, Love and Wisdom
Of the Angels of the Heavenly Father,
So they shall carry us
To the Heavenly Sea.
But if they be stained
With corruption, hatred and ignorance,
They shall chain our feet
To pillars of pain and suffering.
No man can serve two masters;
Neither can evil thoughts abide in a mind
Filled with the Light of the Law.
He who hath found peace with the mind
Hath learned to soar beyond
The Realm of the Angels.
Know this peace with thy mind,
Desire this peace with thy heart,
Fulfill this peace with thy body.

Blessed is the Child of Light
Who is pure in heart,
For he shall see God.
For as the Heavenly Father hath given thee
His holy spirit,
And thy Earthly Mother hath given thee
Her holy body,

So shall ye give love
To all thy brothers.
And thy true brothers are all those
Who do the will of they Heavenly Father
And thy Earthly Mother.
Let thy love be as the sun
Which shines on all the creatures of the earth,
And does not favor one blade of grass
For another.
And this love shall flow as a fountain
From brother to brother,
And as it is spent,
So shall it be replenished.
For love is eternal.
Love is stronger
Than the currents of deep waters.
Love is stronger than death.
And if a man hath not love,
He doth build a wall between him
And all the creatures of the earth,
And therein doth he dwell
In loneliness and pain.
Or he may become as an angry whirlpool
Which sucks into its depths
All that floats too near.
For the heart is a sea with mighty waves,
And love and wisdom must temper it,
As the warm sun breaks through the clouds
And quiets the restless sea.
He who hath found peace with his brothers
Hath entered the kingdom of Love,
And shall see God face to face.
Know this peace with thy mind,
Desire this peace with thy heart,
Fulfill this peace with thy body.

Blessed is the Child of Light
Who doth build on earth
The kingdom of heaven,
For he shall dwell in both worlds.
Thou shalt follow the Law
Of the Brotherhood,

Which saith that none shall have wealth,
And none shall be poor,
And all shall work together
In the garden of the Brotherhood.
Yet each shall follow his own path,
And each shall commune with his own heart.
For in the Infinite Garden
There are many and diverse flowers:
Who shall say that one is best
Because its color is purple,
Or that one is favored
Because its stalk is long and slender?
Though the brothers
Be of different complexion,
Yet do they all toil
In the vineyard of the Earthly Mother,
And they all do lift their voices together
In praise of the Heavenly Father.
And together they break the holy bread,
And in silence share the holy meal
Of thanksgiving.
There shall be no peace among peoples
Till there be one garden of the brotherhood
Over the earth.
For how can there be peace
When each man pursueth his own gain
And doth sell his soul into slavery?
Thou, Child of Light,
Do ye gather with thy brothers
And then go ye forth
To teach the ways of the Law
To those who would hear.
He who hath found peace
With the brotherhood of man
Hath made himself
The co-worker of God.
Know this peace with thy mind,
Desire this peace with thy heart,
Fulfill this peace with thy body.

Blessed is the Child of Light
Who doth study the Book of the Law,
For he shall be as a candle
In the dark of night,
And an island of truth
In a sea of falsehood.
For know ye, that the written word
Which cometh from God
Is a reflection of the Heavenly Sea,
Even as the bright stars
Reflect the face of heaven.
As the words of the Ancient Ones
Are etched with the hand of God
On the Holy Scrolls,
So is the Law engraved on the hearts
Of the faithful who do study them.
For it was said of old,
That in the beginning there were giants
In the earth,
And mighty men which were of old,
Men of renown.
And the Children of Light
Shall guard and preserve
Their written word,
Lest we become again as beasts,
And know not the Kingdom of the Angels.

Know ye, too,
That only through the written word
Shalt thou find that Law
Which is unwritten,
As the spring which floweth from the ground
Hath a hidden source
In the secret depths beneath the earth.
The written Law
Is the instrument by which
The unwritten Law is understood,
As the mute branch of a tree
Becomes a singing flute
In the hands of the shepherd.

Many there are
Who would stay in the tranquil
Valley of ignorance,
Where children play
And butterflies dance in the sun
For their short hour of life.
But none can tarry there long,
And ahead rise the somber
Mountains of learning.
Many there are
Who fear to cross,
And many there are
Who have fallen bruised and bleeding
From their steep and rugged slopes.
But faith is the guide
Over the gaping chasm,
And perseverance the foothold
In the jagged rocks.
Beyond the icy peaks of struggle
Lies the peace and beauty
Of the Infinite Garden of Knowledge,
Where the meaning of the Law
Is made known to the Children of Light.
Here in the center of its forest
Stands the Tree of Life,
Mystery of mysteries.
He who hath found peace
With the teachings of the Ancients,
Through the light of the mind,
Through the light of nature,
And through the study of the Holy Word,
Hath entered the cloud-filled
Hall of the Ancients,
Where dwelleth the Holy Brotherhood,
Of whom no man may speak.
Know this peace with thy mind,
Desire this peace with thy heart,
Fulfill this peace with thy body.

Blessed is the Child of Light
Who knoweth his Earthly Mother,
For she is the giver of life.

Know that thy Mother is in thee,
And thou art in her.
She bore thee
And she giveth thee life.
She it was who gaveth thee thy body,
And to her shalt thou one day
Give it back again.
Know that the blood which runs in thee
Is born of the blood
Of thy Earthly Mother.
Her blood falls from the clouds,
Leaps up from the womb of the earth,
Babbles in the brooks of the mountains,
Flows wide in the rivers of the plains,
Sleeps in the lakes,
Rages mightily in the tempestuous seas.
Know that the air which thou dost breathe
Is born of the breath
Of thy Earthly Mother.
Her breath is azure
In the heights of the heavens,
Soughs in the tops of the mountains,
Whispers in the leaves of the forest,
Billows over the cornfields,
Slumbers in the deep valleys,
Burns hot in the desert.
Know that the hardness of thy bones
Is born of the bones
Of thy Earthly Mother,
Of the rocks and of the stones.
Know that the tenderness of thy flesh
Is born of the flesh
Of thy Earthly Mother,
She whose flesh waxeth yellow and red
In the fruits of the trees.
The light of thy eyes,
The hearing of thy ears,
These are born
Of the colors and the sounds
Of thy Earthly Mother,
Which doth enclose thee about,
As the waves of the sea enclose a fish,

As the eddying air a bird.
I tell thee in truth,
Man is the Son
Of the Earthly Mother,
And from her did the Son of Man
Receive his whole body,
Even as the body of the newborn babe
Is born of the womb of his mother.
I tell thee truly,
Thou art one with the Earthly Mother;
She is in thee, and thou art in her.
Of her wert thou born,
In her dost thou live,
And to her shalt thou return again.
Keep, therefore, her laws,
For none can live long,
Neither be happy,
But he who honors his Earthly Mother
And keepeth her laws.
For thy breath is her breath,
Thy blood her blood,
Thy bone her bone,
Thy flesh her flesh,
Thy eyes and thy ears
Are her eyes and her ears.
He who hath found peace
With his Earthly Mother
Shall never know death.
Know this peace with thy mind,
Desire this peace with thy heart,
Fulfill this peace with thy body.

Blessed is the Child of Light
Who doth seek his Heavenly Father,
For he shall have eternal life.
He that dwelleth in the secret place
Of the Most High
Shall abide under the shadow
Of the Almighty.
For he shall give his Angels charge over thee,
To keep thee in all thy ways.
Know ye that the Lord hath been

Our dwelling place
In all generations.
Before the mountains were brought forth,
Or ever he had formed
The earth and the world,
Even from everlasting to everlasting,
Hath there been love
Between the Heavenly Father
And his children.
And how shall this love be severed?
From the beginning
Until the ending of time
Doth the holy flame of love
Encircle the heads
Of the Heavenly Father
And the Children of Light:
How then shall this love be extinguished?
For not as a candle doth it burn,
Nor yet as a fire raging in the forest.
Lo, it burneth with the flame
Of Eternal Light,
And that flame cannot be consumed.

Ye that love thy Heavenly Father,
Do ye then his bidding:
Walk ye with his Holy Angels,
And find thy peace with his Holy Law.
For his Law is the entire Law:
Yea, it is the Law of laws.
Through his Law he hath made
The earth and the heavens to be one;
The mountains and the sea
Are his footstools.
With his hands he hath made us
And fashioned us,
And he gaveth us understanding
That we may learn his Law.
He is covered with Light
As with a garment:
He stretcheth out the heavens
Like a curtain.

He maketh the clouds his chariot;
He walketh upon the wings of the wind.
He sendeth the springs into the valleys,
And his breath is in the mighty trees.
In his hand are the deep places of the earth:
The strength of the hills is his also.
The sea is his,
And his hands formed the dry land.
All the heavens declare the Glory of God,
And the firmament showeth his Law.
And to his children
Doth he bequeath his Kingdom,
To those who walk with his Angels,
And find their peace with his Holy Law.

Wouldst thou know more, my children?
How may we speak with our lips
That which cannot be spoken?
It is like a pomegranate eaten by a mute:
How then may he tell of its flavor?
If we say the Heavenly Father
Dwelleth within us,
Then are the heavens ashamed;
If we say he dwelleth without us,
It is falsehood.
The eye which scanneth the far horizon
And the eye which seeth the hearts of men
He maketh as one eye.
He is not manifest,
He is not hidden.
He is not revealed,
Nor is he unrevealed.
My children, there are no words
To tell that which he is!
Only this do we know:
We are his children,
And he is our Father.
He is our God,
And we are the children of his pasture,
And the sheep of his hand.
He who hath found peace
With his Heavenly Father

Hath entered the Sanctuary
Of the Holy Law,
And hath made a convenant with God
Which shall endure forever.
Know this peace with thy mind,
Desire this peace with thy heart,
Fulfill this peace with thy body.
Though heaven and earth may pass away,
Not one letter of the Holy Law
Shall change or pass away.
For in the beginning was the Law,
And the Law was with God,
And the Law was God.
May the Sevenfold Peace
Of the Heavenly Father
Be with thee always.

From *The Essene Book of Jesus*

The Bodhisattva Vow

JANG CHUB NYING POR CHI KYI BAR
SANGE NAMLA KYABSU CHI
CHO DANG JANG CHUB SEM PA YI
TSOK LANG DE SHIN KYAB SU CHI
JI TAR NGON GYI DE SHEK KYI
JANG CHUB TUK NI KYE PA DANG
JANG CHUB SEMPAI LAB PA LA
DE DAK RIM SHIN NE PA TAR
DE SHIN DRO LA PEN DON DU
JANG CHUB SEM NI KYE GYI SHING
DE SHIN DU NI LAB PA LANG
RIM PA SHIN DU LAB PAR GYI
(*Repeat three times*)

DENG DU DAK TSI DRU BU YO
MI YI SA PA LEK PAR TOB
DE RING SANGYE RIK SU KYE
SANGYE SE SU DAK DENG GYUR
DA NI DAK GI CHI NE KYANG
RIK DANG TUNPAE LAY TSAM DE
KYÖNME TSUNPAE RIK DI LA
NYOK PAR MI GYUR DE TAR JA
DAK GI DE RNIG KYOBPA TAMCHAY KYI
CHEN NGAR DROWA DE SHEK NI DANG NI
PAR DU DE LA DRÖNDU BÖ SIN GYI
LA DANG LA MIN LA SOK GA WAR GYI
JANG CHUB SEM NI RINPOCHE
MA KYE BA NAM KYE GYUR CHIK
KYEPA NYAMPA ME PA DANG
GONG NE GONG DU PEL WAR SHOK
JANG CHUB SEM DANG MI DREL SHING
JANG CHUB CHÖ LA SHÖL WA DANG
SANGYE NAM KYI YONG SUNG SHING
DÜ KYI LAY NAM PONG WAR SHO
JANG CHUB SEMPA NAM KYI NI
DRO DÜN TUK LA GONG DRUB SHO
GÖN PO YI NI GANG GONG PA
SEM CHEN NAM LA DE JOR SHOK
SEM CHEN TAM CHE DE DANG DEN GYUR CHIK
NGEN DRO TAM CHAY TAK TU TONG PAR SHO
JANG CHUB SEM PA GANG DAK SAR SHUK PA
DAY DAK DUN GYI MÖN LAM DRUB PAR SHOK

SEM CHEN TAM CHAY DAY WA DANG
DAYWAE GYU
DANG DEN PAR GYUR CHIK
DUK NGEL DANG DUK NGEL GYI GYU
DANG DRAL WAR GYUR CHIK
DUK NGEL MAY PAY DAYWA DAM PA
DANG MI DRALWAR GYUR CHIK
NYERING CHAK DANG DANG
DRALWAE TANG NYOM CHEN
PO LA NAY PAR GYUR CHIK.
(*Repeat three times*)

Until the heart of enlightenment is reached I take refuge in all the Buddhas, and in all the teachings and the Bodhisattvas. Just as all the former Buddhas generated the thought of enlightenment (Bodhicitta) in themselves, and went through the Bodhisattva development, the six liberating virtues, so I also will generate the thought of enlightenment and, step by step, develop myself into a Bodhisattva for the sake of all beings.
(*Repeat three times*)

I now have a fruitful life. I have obtained a precious human body. I have been born into the family of Buddha and become a son of Buddha. I promise to live in accordance with this family and do nothing that will stain this noble and flawless lineage.

Today before the eyes of all those in whom we take refuge, I invite all sentient beings to tread the path to Buddhahood with me and to be happy. All gods, demi-gods and all the inhabitants of the six realms rejoice! May the thought of enlightenment be developed in those who do not have it and may it never weaken those who have, but continually increase. May I never be removed from the thought of enligthenment like all the Bodhisattvas, and may I, with their help and support, avoid all negative actions and practice the Bodhisattva conduct. May all the thoughts that the Bodhisattvas think for the sake of all sentient beings be fulfilled.

May all beings enjoy happiness and the causes of happiness. May they be removed from suffering and the causes of suffering. May they never be removed from the highest bliss which is freedom from suffering. May they rest in great harmony, not loving those closest to themselves while feeling aversion to others, but feeling the same deep love for all sentient beings.
(*Repeat three times*)

Ceremony of Peace

Peace comes to me most fully when I can realize the perfection of the unfolding moment and focus on Now, on the wholeness which is the truth underlying the separation and conflict we are playing out in the physical world, on the holiness that lives within me and all things. Long ago the mysterious holy woman, White Buffalo Calf Pipe Woman, brought our Lakota people the reminder of Creator's Law of Oneness. She reminded us that each day is a holy day, each step upon sacred ground, and that the Great Spirit lives within us and all things in the circle of life at all times. Walking a holy way or 'walking in a sacred manner' means moving through our days holding in our attention the fact that we are all a part of the web of life, and are all sacred beings.

To bring myself into present moment awareness of this oneness/wholeness/holiness, I have a special personal practice which involves a chant or meditation upon the name of God, Creator, All That Is, rather than allowing my mind to roam about with internal chatter which is meaningless, limiting, or downright negative. The first part is a releasing, letting-go, a de-structing of *everything* in my experience – a complete clearing of all the past, whether ideas, beliefs, images, names, experiences. This is important, because what is true and necessary will remain with me, and what is not will be cleansed. I experience this cleansing like a washing of mind, body, emotions, spirit, which leaves only a complete blackness or void. I close my eyes and go deeply into that void during this beginning stage.

The second part of the meditation/chant, in contrast, is a total celebration of things *exactly as they are in this moment*. I begin by a joyful celebration of myself, just as I am right now – not as I was a few minutes or days or years ago, not as I would ideally like to be, not as I will become, but perfect in the moment exactly as I am. Then I softly and gradually open my eyes, celebrating the things closest to me, and then further and further out in the ring of my sight. Then the celebration and love and acceptance are extended to pour over the whole country, the whole world, All That Is, exactly as it is right now. Then the cycle returns, where I let go of all I experience, release the present, clear away all conceptions, and embrace the void again. This cycle is a profound way to begin the day.

BROOKE MEDICINE EAGLE

On our altar, we have a peace candle. In the daily lighting of this candle, we offer this prayer:

In Lighting the Candle

O Great Mother of Peace,
in the names of your children
and the children of your children
we light this candle
in remembrance, in gratitude,
in reverence and in hounor of
You.

O Holy Mother,
O Spiritual Mother
of the Divine Spark of Light
that you ignite and reflect
in our souls,
be here now.

We are called the Peacemakers.
Blessed are our ways.
We are known as the true children
of Divine Love and Divine Wisdom,
your spiritual children on Earth.

O Great Mother,
gather all of your children and
grace us with
Peace on Earth now.   *Amena**

In Extinguishing the Candle

O Holy Sophia,
May the sacred smoke
from your Light
cover the Earth like a mist.

May all the people and nations
be under your influence and power
so that we might understand
the true meaning of Love
and fulfill our dream of
Peace on Earth now.   *Amena**

Amen is the Hebrew word usually used at the end of prayers and means 'truly'.
Amena is a derivative of an Arabic word which means 'to make complete'.
   Since the Divine Feminine is what we feel is lacking to make the world complete,
Amena is used at the end of our prayers.   AURORA TERRENUS
                                                    (Holy Order of Wisdom)

The Weaver's Song

Background
In 1973 I had the inspiration to write words and music for a short song, which is the basis of the ceremony for Peace which follows shortly. It involves the sacred Directions of the Planet, East, South, West, North, Above, Below and Within. At the time of writing the song, it appeared as a waking dream, in which a man from an ancestral megalithic culture was lying on his back in the centre of a stone circle, attuning to the Directions, the stars, sky and earth.

Some years passed before I realised the wealth of meaning and vast tradition behind my vision of the sacred Directions and the sacred land and planet. Such traditions have their variants worldwide in every culture, and represent a truth, something to which we are now beginning to return, at a time of great need for simple powerful truths. I recorded the 'Weaver's Song' in several different arrangements, and performed it many times on tour. The heart of the words, however, can be opened out into a non-denominational circling ceremony for Peace, focussing upon the riddle of the last line: 'Peace is a secret unknown'.

The Weaving Ritual: A Ceremonial Circle for Peace
This may be conducted by any number of people, who are each allocated roles around the circle.

People (*see diagram showing the four directions of the circle*)
East
South
West
North
The Opener of Gates: North-east and Centre
Further people are aligned according to each Direction.

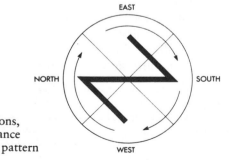

The Directions,
the circle dance
and the 'Z' pattern

1   The ceremony begins in silence, each of the four Directions holding a candle. All present turn their attention inwards towards peace.

2   **Opener**   Peace is a secret unknown.
    All   Still are the voices that echoed alone.
    Opener   Open the Gates of the Star-ways.
    (*Lights candle or flame in centre*)
    All   Gone are the places of whispering stones.

3   **Opener**   From one thread of light are all words and all worlds woven
And no single part is severed from the whole:
Let us summon the power of the Weaver here among us,
According to the pattern of the mystery.
(*Takes taper, lights it from central flame and then passes it to* **East**)

4   **East**   (*Lights Eastern flame with taper*)
I call upon the power of the East
To awaken and attend through this blessed Gate:
By the power of Air,
By the power of Dawn,
By the power of Life.
(*Hands taper to* **South,** *who lights Southern flame*)

5   **South**   I call upon the power of the South
To arise and attend through this blessed Gate:
By the power of Fire,
By the power of bright Noonday,
By the power of Light.
(*Hands taper to* **West,** *who lights Western flame*)

6   **West**   I call upon the power of the West
To increase and attend through this blessed Gate:
By the power of Water,
By the power of Sunset,
By the power of Love.
(*Hands taper to* **North,** *who lights Northern flame*)

7   **North**   I call upon the power of the North
To appear and attend through this blessed Gate:
In the name of the power of Earth,

By the power of the Mirror of Stars,
By the power of Law and Liberty.

8   All resonate HUM, AUM or AMEN, according to choice, and focus attention upon the central light.

9   *East*   Now for you I weave some weaving;
Listen to it well.
Now for you I twist some twining;
Listen to its spell:

10   *All*   Once I was held in the eyes of the night,
(*Arms raised in the sign of Stars*)
Once in the voice of the Day,
(*Arms held out level in the sign of the Sun*)
Once in the arms of a child alone,
(*Arms crossed in the sign of Humanity*)
And once in the mind of a stone.
(*Arms held downwards in the sign of the Earth*)

11   *East*   In and in the words are weaving
Through these eyes so blind;
Through and through you hold my weaving
In your own design.
(*Pauses before proceeding:*)

12   *East*   Once I gained a seed from the Dawn,
South   Once the jewel from a nest,
North   Once the light from a fair lady's mirror,
West   Once a word from the West.

13   *West*   Now it is ending,
Slow your breathing,
Now your joys are mine;
Through and through you hold my weaving
In your own design.

14   *All*   Gone are the places of whispering stones,
Open the Gates of the Star-ways,
Still are the voices that echoed alone,
Peace is a secret unknown.

15   The Opener chants AMEN; all chant AMEN (or resonate HUM or AUM).

16 A circle dance begins, led by East (if space permits): all except the Opener move East/South/West/North, awakening to the energies of each Quarter as they pass.

17 The Opener allows the energies to build as required, then strikes a gong or claps his/her hands three times. East now changes the direction of the dance to pass East/South/North/West three times. After third 'Z' movement, all return sunwise (clockwise) to their original positions.

18 All pause here for silent meditation.

19 The Opener extinguishes the central light, using the Crossing Formula as follows:

> In the name of the Star Father,
> The Earth Mother,
> The True Taker,
> The Great Giver,
> One Being of Light.

20 All resonate HUM, AUM or AMEN and depart in silence.

R. J. STEWART

Honouring the Divine Wisdom

Challenging Humanity to Follow the Way

Six persons stand in a circle, each holding a candle. A large candle is placed in the centre. A seventh person, holding a lit taper, enters the circle, and before lighting the solitary candle, proclaims, along with the six: 'Does not Wisdom call out: "I raise my voice to all humanity: Walk with me in the way of Righteousness; along the paths of Justice."'

All stand in silence; the seventh person declares: 'Knowledge of the Holy One is understanding,' and proceeds to light the six candles in turn. In the sanctuary, on an altar or table, are kept copies of the world's Scriptures. Near by are six candlesticks or a candelabra. In silence, each of the six leaves the circle in turn and places his/her candle on the altar, returning to the circle with a copy of one of the holy books. When all six have returned, the seventh declares: 'By Love is Wisdom seen; in Love is Wisdom known; for Love is Wisdom manifested in our lives.'

Following a period of silence, portions are read from each of the Scriptures in turn, depending on the festival or theme chosen. The Scriptures are then taken back to the sanctuary and the six persons return to the circle to hold hands.

The seventh reads from *The Way of Life* (54):

> Cultivate The Way yourself; and your virtue will be genuine;
> Cultivate it in your home; and its virtue will overflow;
> Cultivate it in your village; and your village will prosper;
> Cultivate it in your country; and your nation will flourish;
> Cultivate it in the whole world; and virtue will be universal.

The seventh person shares the Kiss of Peace with the six, who then exchange it with one another; he or she leaves the circle and extinguishes the six candles. Before the seven persons blow out the solitary candle together, they declare: 'Seek good and not evil; establish justice and let it flow like water; righteousness, like an everflowing stream.'

GERAINT AP IORWERTH
(Order of Sancta Sophia)

Pax Deae: The Peace of the Goddess

Peace, being a oneness,
An act as well as a state of mind,
Wave and shore,
Motion and stillness,
Not static, not carved in stone,
Eternal in its motion,
Not its durability.

By making a sacred act we enter the *Pax Deae*. This act can turn even a mundane and everyday object or thought into something holy and special. It reminds us that everything is sacred and that nothing should be despised.

When all was ready, the celebrants entered the sacred space, carrying offerings of barley, wine, water and incense. They proceeded to the altar. There a fire was kindled and consecrated. A circle was marked out around the altar; the celebrants carried the offerings and incense three times around the circle in a sunwise direction. Thus was the sacred space delineated and separated from the everyday world.

The chief celebrant poured water over the hands of the participants, purifying them for the coming act. After this came silence. This holy silence could have lasted for eternity, but it was broken by the chant, the mantra, which was repeated three times, then three times again, onwards and upwards. Gathering all together, becoming the single song, in this sacred place between the worlds the unity unfolded.

This symbolic gathering-together became the primal task before the sacrifice or offering. It mirrored and re-enacted creation. All things flowed from the Creatrix before being offered back to her in a sacred act, by which all things themselves became sacred. It reinforced the unity that interweaves all things. Therefore, in the act of worship, the whole universe took part. We became the single song, in concert with the Goddess. As the flame within all burned brighter, everything was renewed, made fresh, and brought closer to the One.

After the chant came the prayer, the offering and the libation to the Goddess. The act was done. All had entered the irreversible, bloodless and gentle peace of the Goddess. All had returned new-made.

STUART LITTLEJOHN

A Ceremony of Peace

To be at peace we need not only to be at peace within ourselves but with all of the universe.

First find a place; this could be a garden, park or the wild. It should be a place where there are trees, plants, stones and rocks, and which is visited by animals and birds. Before enacting the ceremony, visit the place and note the natural surroundings in order to familiarise yourself with them. Decide on a journey or path around the area that you have chosen, so that you can sit with a tree or a plant; then select a place where you can see birds and where you can be with a rock or a stone.

When you are ready to perform the ceremony, choose a day when you are not hurried for time. You need to take with you a rattle or a percussion instrument and an offering to the place. This could be seeds for the birds and earth.

On the way to the place on the day of the ceremony, think about peace and how you would like to be more peaceful. Start the ceremony at the beginning of your path with a dedication and statement of what you would like to occur by performing the ceremony. Repeat this dedication three times. An example could be: 'On this day I have come to make peace with the tree, the birds and the moss-covered stone. I have come to learn from these sacred powers what wisdom they have for achieving greater peace and harmony in the world.' Then leave your gift at the beginning of your path.

Start shaking your rattle as you walk towards the tree or first chosen object of sacred power. When you arrive at the tree, sit down and listen to the peace that it embodies. Be silent with the tree and become at one with it. As you sit quietly, let the voice of the tree come into your head and ask how you can be at peace with the tree. Ask the tree how you might bring peace to the world.

When you have heard the wisdom of the tree, give thanks by shaking the rattle and continue shaking it to a place where you can see the birds. Find somewhere where you can either see them in the branches or in the sky. Sit down and allow your spirit to contact theirs, as you did with the tree. Ask how you, and then how the world, can be at peace with the birds. Again, when you have finished, rattle your thanks and continue shaking the rattle to the stone.

Repeat the questions and rattle your thanks to the stone.

When you have the messages from the tree, bird and stone, put them together in a sentence. Find a place on the path in which you can feel the peace of nature. Sit here and spread the message that you have received via meditation or contemplation to all the earth and its inhabitants. Feel the web of all the others that are working for peace and add your thoughts to theirs.

Thank the tree, bird and stone again by shaking the rattle, and leave by walking back along the path the way you came.

This ceremony can be changed and adapted according to the place chosen; for instance, you can ask the wisdom of a river or pond, a flower or hill. Try different things and see what works for you.

Peace comes from being in harmony with one's surroundings. The ceremony outlined above can be extended to listening to the wisdom of the house that you live in and the place in which that house is. All things have a spirit with which we can live in peace.

FELICITY WOMBWELL

Tread the inner spiral to
find the heart of peace

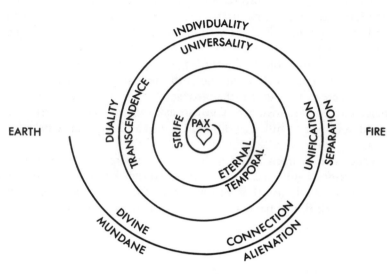

AIR

EARTH

FIRE

WATER

NAOMI OZANIEC

The Inner Chamber of Peace

The human heart, indeed your heart and mine, is the divine organ for Peace. In a world of change and turmoil, each of us could deliberately create a focal point of light and love. That is what Christ calls on us to achieve.

The human heart can go the lengths of God.

Christopher Fry

Create that inner chamber of stillness.

Put aside busy, disturbing thoughts.

Let the chapel of the soul be flooded with serenity and tranquillity.

Love all life. Know that you are not entitled, as a human being, to pass judgement or criticise any other being: 'Judge not, that ye be not judged' (St Matthew, 7:1); 'Be still then, and know that I am God' (Psalms, 46:9).

You can, if you choose, deliberately cut out from your vocabulary all words of fear, doubt, hate, anger, criticism, cynicism. You can jettison them and decide never to use them again. This is a constructive deed leading inevitably to soul change and inner stillness, thus creating a setting into which Peace and love for all life can manifest themselves. This is your vital contribution in a planet of free choice. It is a creative deed of deliberate co-operation with the ever-present Divinity in the soul. Active Peace would then move over the planet.

The Earth faces the changes. Much that is negative must be swept away in the process. But we can each choose to make ourselves a focal point of peace and love for the channelling of the Light. Our higher selves and angelic guides will assuredly be very close, and the souls who have mastered inner tranquillity will be lifted and blended in the rising tide of love which now begins to flood the planet. The deed of Peace is inner volition, which each can offer to God.

Seeke out ye goode in everie man
And speke of all the beste ye can;
Then will all men speke well of thee,
And say how kynde of harte ye be.

Geoffrey Chaucer

SIR GEORGE TREVELYAN

Victory

A Question and an Answer

This is a brief rite, intended to question the validity of *any* war. It may be performed by as few as three people, though it will benefit from the two armies being represented by eighteen or twenty men. Victory may be spoken by a woman or a man.

Victory	Listen, you men who glory in the name of War – I am Victory: the disease of the defeated, the plague of the triumphant. I am more feared than War, and less easy to find than a thread of purple silk in a broad field of thistles.
Both Armies	Yet we seek you.
Victory	Is it me you seek? Or is it the death of Fear that you long for?
First Army	We seek the Victory!
Second Army	We seek the Victory!
First Army	We will take the blood of our enemies and trample it into your lustrous wings.
Second Army	We will smear the blood of our enemies on the scented flesh of your thighs.
First Army	We will open the gates of iron and bronze, and release the wine-red flood, that our enemies may drown in it.
Second Army	We will sow the forgetful poppy in the wounded fields, that the names of our enemies may be obliterated.
Both Armies	And our names shall live for ever!
Victory	What are your names? *(Silence)*
Victory	What use are your wreathed names, given in unspeaking stone? What solemn melody greets your triumph, other than the dirge of the dead and the angry silence of the defeated? What embrace will greet your returning, but the clasp of Death, sighing with deep satisfaction as she gathers you to her hollow bosom?
First Army	But Victory should spread before us the feast of feasts!
Second Army	But Victory should usher in the lithe-limbed dancers with garlands and kisses!

Both Armies	Where are the crowds, the cheering, the replenishment of joys?
	(Silence)
First Army	Is there nothing but silence?
Second Army	Is there nothing but silence?
Victory	In the silence comes the question: do you long for War because you fear Love?
	(Silence. The armies kneel)
Victory	Fear dwells in men like a parasitic worm, feeding on virtue, poisoning the blood with its excrement of envy and hate.
	Rid yourselves of Fear. Arise. With eyes and arms and open hearts, embrace your brothers.
	(The armies stand; they embrace each other. Music, if desired)
Victory	The true Victory is the Triumph of Love. Go out into the world, truly victorious, and let ten thousand years of peace and plenty come upon the Earth.
	Let the surly hinges of the shut doors of the Temple of War rust to immobility. Let us go together to the open precinct of the Temple of Concord.
	May this, our turning sanctuary, be known throughout the universe as the Planet of Peace.

PHILIP LE GALOISE

The Oblation of the World

Let my mind be still, emptied of all thought of self, that in quietness and humility I may bring before You, my Lord, the totality of the life of the earth.

May my heart, cleansed by Your transforming Fire, be a pure altar on which I may offer to You all the labour and sorrow of mankind.

On the paten of my heart I would place, O my Lord, the purposeful action of men, their aspirations, their achievements, their work. Into my chalice I would pour the sorrows, the failings and the pain of every living being.

Into this oblation of the whole world I would gather, first, those closest to me, those whose lives are bound up with my own personal life, those known to me, especially those whom I love.

With these may I unite those more distant and unreal to me, the whole anonymous mass of humankind, scattered in every corner of the globe. In sympathy and imagination I would unite myself with the ceaseless pilgrimage of mankind, with its joys and sorrows, its hopes and fears, its successes and failures, that I may be one with it all.

Let every sentient being be placed upon the altar of my heart, that I may raise them all up to You.

And not only the living would I gather into this oblation, but also the dead, that they too may be incorporated into the material of my sacrifice.

It is not enough. I would draw into it every form of life, animals and birds, reptiles and insects, trees, flowers, and all the kindly fruits of the earth. Let these too be laid upon this inner altar, that they too may be offered to You.

And yet the oblation is incomplete. Into it I would draw the very fabric of the earth itself, the material substance of which it is composed, that I may present nothing less than everything to You who are the All-in-all.

Creative Power, shining, deathless, Spirit, wherein lay hidden the earth and all its creatures, so infuse this Your world with Your attraction that it may more and more be led back into You from whence it sprang.

Timeless Word, outpouring of the essence of the mysterious ineffable One, made flesh for us in the Lord Jesus, You who are ever moulding this manifold, phenomenal world so as to incorporate it more and more into Your divine life, You who are ever plunging Yourself into its depth and totality so as to touch us through everything within and without us, breathe into it now, Your transforming might. You who are Life and Giver of life.

May all my life, past, present and future, that which was, that which is, and that which is to come, be now elevated at the altar to my heart, that in and through You, O eternal, cosmic Christ, it may now be presented, a holy sacrifice, in the secret place of the Most High, that all may be hallowed and consecrated unto that great Day of the final redemption of the whole creation, when this corruptible shall put on incorruption and this mortal shall put on immortality, and all things shall, in and through You, be brought back into the One from whence they came.

Now over the whole earthly pilgrimage of mankind (and over me, over us) pronounce Your revealing, consubstantial words, words of consecration, and also the annunciation of the ultimate mystery of the universe and of ourselves:

THIS IS MY BODY

THIS IS MY BLOOD

It is done. The oblation and the consecration are made. Grant us Your Peace.

F. C. HAPPOLD

Absolute Bodhicitta

We must consider self-love and egotism to be our worst enemies. We should also take all fellow beings as our best friends and render them our assistance. However, we do not as yet have the ability to put this into practice. Therefore, our first goal must be to train our mind accordingly. Let us now be determined to repay the love of all our former mothers and fathers (as embodied in all beings). It should be our aim to help them and to satisfy all their needs. They themselves strive for happiness. By rewarding them with our love, we exercise our mind in the method known as giving and taking. In practice, however, taking comes first. For example, if we want to fill a dish with good food, we must clean it first. Likewise, we should be resolutely prepared to take upon ourselves the sorrows of all beings. We should regard their sufferings as black rays which approach us from the ten directions and which then enter into us. Then we must develop the determination to give happiness, virtue and merit to all living beings. Again, our determination is accompanied by a devout prayer to our object of refuge in order that it may be fulfilled. At this point we visualize rays of light going out to all living beings, bringing them happiness and merit. This exercise should be repeated very frequently.

LAMA SHEREB GYALTSEN AMIPA

Ritual of Reconciliation

This ritual was designed to clear the air by giving voice to the unspoken emotions that fuelled hostility, and was originally enacted by the representatives of two groups who had seemingly irreconcilable differences. It could also be used where a quarrel is personal, with those caught in the crossfire participating and sharing their own feelings about the situation.

As part of the preparations for meeting in ritual space, find a ball of wool in a colour that conveys peacemaking to you, and fill a basket or tray with seasonal gleanings; appropriate correspondences will occur to you, but they might include nettles for stinging remarks, rue for bitterness, brambles for feeling ensnared, dead wood for things to be cleared, olive branches for peace and seed heads for hope.

The participants gather in a close circle, sitting comfortably, the basket of gleanings in the centre. Explain the nature and purpose of the occasion using words prepared in advance or as the spirit moves you at that moment.

Each person winds the wool round one wrist, saying why he or she is there, and passes the ball on. When the first circle is complete, one person selects a gleaning to represent how he/she is feeling (such as a holy sprig for prickliness or irritability), ties this to the wool, while speaking from the heart, and then passes the thread across the circle. This is repeated several times by each participant, the web being knotted at crossing points, until many truths have been spoken and all hearts are unburdened. If it feels appropriate, you might sing or chant together.

Open the circle and release the web, adorned with the symbols of shared griefs, pain, anger, peace offerings, hope, in whatever way seems right. Share a meal together.

SEREN WILDWOOD

Binding the Wolf

A Peace Ritual in the Norse Tradition

(*The group gathers together; agrees on a list of evils that destroy peace and lists them on a piece of paper; casts a circle as desired; and lights a red candle and dragon's blood incense. The Leader chants:*)

Tyr, hear our summons! Undefeated defender and Lord of the All-
   Thing, come to aid us now!
As Fenris thou didst feed, of the Beast thou wert binder,
One-hand – thus winning reknown – bless thou our battle!
These are the evils we oppose –
(*The Leader reads the list of evils to be neutralised*)
Hear and help us now to bind them!

With what shall we bind the wolves of war?
What powers preserve the peace we long for?
This frail cord I bless for binding –
The power of _____ I set upon it!
Small though it seem, its spirit is mighty,
By _____ shall Fenris be bound!

(*Each participant takes a length of thread, and names a power that can neutralise one of the evils stated above. The Leader gathers the threads and twists them into a cord, with which he/she ties the paper on which the evils have been written, while all chant:*)
The fetter is fast and Fenris bound!

(*The Leader lights the tied paper and lets it burn*)
Fire consume all evil here,
Fire shall free us all from fear,
As this gyve is tightly wound,
Earth shall hold what we have bound!

(*All chant:*)
Tyr, we praise thee on this day,
Protection grant from those who slay;
Mars and Morrigan, Durga, Din,
Bind the wolves without, within!

(*The ceremony finishes with the sharing of food and drink. The circle is uncast as desired, and the ashes of the paper are buried at a crossroads*)

DIANA PAXSON

Peace of the Mother God

Rainbow Network of the Fellowship of Isis

Members and friends of the Fellowship of Isis assemble round a family hearth during a fellowship attunement time.

Priestess of Isis	Holy Goddess Isis of Ten Thousand Names, Mother of all beings, come to our hearts! Grant us, Thy children, of whatever race, religion and country, Peace on earth and within ourselves.
Priest of Isis	Companions, we are assembled here at the Hearth Fire of the Mother God, in attunement with our Iseums all over the world, in order to attain Peace and to send it forth.
First Companion	(*Anoints each brow with water*) May you receive true vision of your future way, that you may bring peace with understanding!
Second Companion	(*Lights a taper from the fire and hands it to each person*) Feel love in your heart, for without love you may not attain Peace and joy!
Priestess	Let us form a circle and, with uplifted hands, feel love, joy and Peace in our hearts! (*All turn inwards and may feel a glow within and see coloured auras around the circle*)
Priest	May we now turn outwards and send forth rays of Peace to all beings born of the Mother! (*All turn outwards and send forth rays of Peace, which may be seen as coloured shafts of light*)

Priestess   Companions, let us experience silent communion with the Deities. (*Silence is maintained by all for about twenty minutes. Reports are given of any inspiration felt or visions experienced. All rise, and the Priestess resumes:*) In the Name of the Goddess Isis of Ten Thousand Names (*makes the sign of Ankh*), may all beings be blessed; spirits and humans; animals, birds, reptiles and insects; trees and plants; and every element.

Priest   We give thanks to the Mother Goddess for divine Peace within our hearts. Let us celebrate the Feast of Concordia, Salus, Pax! (*The Fourth and Fifth Companions bless the food and drink, and the feast is enjoyed. Offerings are kept aside for the needy, both human and animal*)

OLIVIA ROBERTSON, Priestess Hierophant
(Fellowship of Isis)

As we are together, praying for peace, let us be truly with each other.

Let us pay attention to our breathing.

Let us be relaxed in our bodies and our minds.

Let us be at peace with our bodies and our minds.

Let us return to ourselves and become wholly ourselves. Let us maintain a half-smile on our faces.

Let us be aware of the source of being common to us all and to all living things.

Evoking the presence of the Great Compassion, let us fill our hearts with our own compassion – towards ourselves and towards all living beings.

Let us pray that all living beings realize that they are all brothers and sisters, all nourished from the same source of life.

Let us pray that we ourselves cease to be the cause of suffering to each other.

Let us plead with ourselves to live in a way which will not deprive other beings of air, water, food, shelter, or the chance to live.

With humility, with awareness of the existence of life, and of the sufferings that are going on around us, let us pray for the establishment of peace in our hearts and on earth. Amen

THICH NHAT HANH

Self-Clarification and the Resolution of Conflict

Peace begins at home. Many of us have peaceful intentions to the world at large, but what is the use of feelings of cosmic peace if our own heart is troubled and we cannot keep peace within the family or between neighbours? The following technique of self-clarification may be used in many situations. Our chief duty should be the dissolution of the chains of conflict which keep us embattled. Only then can be call ourselves Peacekeepers.

This can be done each day, before sleeping. Conflict should be set aside as we lie down to rest. Conflict retained is one of the chief causes of insomnia, which itself may lead to difficulties and further conflicts the next day. Answer the following questions truthfully, and please adapt the categories below to suit your own circumstances:

Is there peace between me and my soul?
Is there peace between me and my family?
Is there peace between me and my neighbours?
Is there peace between me and my environment?
Is there peace between me and my country?
Is there peace between my faith and those of others?
Is there peace between my race and those of others?
Is there peace between my generation and those of others?
Is there peace between my country and the world?
Is there peace between me and the Spirit?

Go through this list, perhaps focussing on one particular question each day. Asking this question will spark other questions, such as: 'What causes conflict?'; 'How can peace be effected?'. Hold each group in your heart and pray, letting your breath dissolve any darkness or blockage that stands between you and any other:

May there be peace between me and my soul.
May there be peace between me and my family.
May there be peace between me and my neighbours.
May there be peace between me and my environment.
May there be peace between me and my country.
May there be peace between my faith and all others.
May there be peace between my race and all others.
May there be peace between my generation and all others.
May there be peace between my country and the world.

May there be peace between me and the Spirit, and may the Spirit breathe peace into every breast.

On a practical daily basis, you may find that any conflicts present within yourself will come to a head. Do not attempt to quell this movement. Peace cannot be built upon shaky foundations of wished-for pacification. We cannot for ever go on tip-toeing around areas of our life that are full of conflict. To pray for peace means we have to be actively prepared to deal with conflict.

The resolution of conflict is never simple. The following principles can be borne in mind while we get down to the practical problems:

Conceive that you may be mistaken or see only part of the picture.

Conceive that your opponent may be justified.

Conceive that one side may have to concede more than the other.

Conceive that what is perceived as a negative vice can also work as a positive virtue; for instance, sudden aggression and greed may indicate a nature capable of swift protectiveness and generosity, yet these virtues have never been recognised because the negative aspects have always been labelled 'incurable' or 'unchangeable'.

Conceive of your opponent as a sentient being like yourself; visualise him/her as an innocent child, as an uncertain teenager, as a mature adult, as a wise elder.

Conceive of how your conflict warps the world-web, the great net of life and consciousness which binds us all together.

In resolving conflict, a balance has to be found and the parties concerned have to talk together or use an arbitrator. Let a prayer to resolve conflict be said before such a meeting starts: the Lord's Prayer, the Peace Prayer described above or any suitable format from this book. This disposes all hearts to hearken to the voice of the Spirit, however this is understood.

Let the framework of the situation be rehearsed and both sides heard. Let each side be encouraged to respond positively to the other by the presentation of an action, gift or intention which will make the foundations of a bridge. If no agreement can be reached, let each side agree to rest on the matter and to meet again soon. The arbitrator, especially, must pray hard to find common ground between the groups. If partial agreement is the result, let each side make an exchange of promises and ground these in mutual trust and patience. If full agreement is reached, let each side be very much aware of how much it owes the other and resolve to keep the channels of communication open so that no such conflict will take place in future.

These peace principles can be utilised at any level of human existence, whether it be between child and parent, wife and husband, employee and employer, or between defending and attacking forces. In every case, the seed-bed of peace lies within the ground of each soul.

CAITLÍN MATTHEWS

How to Preserve Within You the Peace of God

If you have felt that your mind has come to be at one with the soul and body, that you are no longer cut into pieces by sin but are something unified and whole, that the hallowed peace of Christ is breathing in you, then watch over this gift of God with all possible care. Let prayer and the reading of religious books be your principal occupation; give to other works only a secondary importance, be cold towards earthly activities, and if possible eschew them altogether. Sacred peace, fine as the breath of the Holy Spirit, immediately withdraws from the soul which behaves carelessly in its presence; the soul which lacks reverence, proves disloyal by indulging in sin, and permits itself to grow negligent. Together with the peace of Christ, grace-given prayer withdraws likewise from the unworthy soul: then the passions invade it like hungry beasts, and begin to torment the victim who has given himself to them, and who has been left to himself by God, who has withdrawn from him. If you become surfeited with food, or still more with drink, the peace of God will cease to act in you. If you are angry, you wil lose this peace for a long while. If you allow yourself to become irreverent, the Holy Spirit will no longer work within you. If you begin to love something earthly, if you become infected by a passionate attachment to some object or skill, or by a special liking for some person, holy peace will certainly withdraw from you. If you allow yourself to take pleasure in impure thoughts, peace will leave you for a long time, because it does not tolerate the evil stench of sin – and especially the sins of lust and vanity. You will seek this peace and find it not; you will weep for its loss; but it will pay no attention to your tears, that so you may learn to give due value to the divine gift, and to guard it with proper care and reverence.

Hate everything that draws you down into distraction or sin. Crucify yourself on the cross of the Gospel commandments; keep yourself always nailed to it. Rebuff all sinful thoughts and wishes with courage and vigilance; cast away earthly cares; try to live the Gospel by zealously fulfilling all its commandments. When you pray, once more crucify yourself on the cross of prayer. Push aside all the memories, however important they may be, which come to you during prayer: ignore every one of them. Do not theologize, do not be carried away by following up brilliant, original, and powerful ideas which suddenly occur to you. Sacred silence, which is induced in the mind at the time of prayer by a sense of God's greatness, speaks of God more profoundly and more eloquently than any human words. 'If you pray truly,' said the Fathers, 'you *are* a theologian.'

BISHOP IGNATII

A Dream of Peace

A Visualisation

You have been travelling all day, and night is fast coming upon you, yet still you are surrounded by high, bare moorland. The sky is overcast and all looks cold and grey, when a beam of escaping sunlight stabs down and reveals to you a hidden vale in which is a cottage surrounded by a beautiful garden, the like of which you have never seen. As there appears to be no path to it, it is only with great difficulty that you manage to scramble down the rock and heather towards it.

As you approach you call softly, but there is no answer. Both cottage and garden seem to be deserted. Drawing nearer, you open the gate and enter the garden. It is as if you enter a different world. The sun still shines, but the air is now warm and scented with the perfume of the luxuriant flowers. These elements, together with the gentle hum of bees and insects, make you realise how tired you are. Sitting down against one of the tall, grey, golden-flowered trees that surround and ring the garden, you fall gradually into a deep sleep, and dream.

In your dream it is early evening, the stars are visible and shine with frozen fire. They are so brilliant that they cast shadows of all that surrounds you. As you look around, you see a path that seems to shimmer and glitter in the starlight, as if it may only be seen by that ethereal light. Watching, you see, dimly at first but then more clearly, a number of beings coming along it towards you. They are like none you have ever seen before.

They are tall, clad in raiment that seems frosted with gems and jewels, which appear to radiate the starlight. Their faces are the most beautiful you have ever seen. They in turn see you and come towards you, smiling. One, golden-haired and taller than the rest, comes closer to you and says, 'Greetings, child of the followers. Pleased are we that you have found this refuge. Here you may ask concerning that which you desire and truly seek.'

You ask for peace and how it may be found.

He looks at you again and replies, 'Ah, that is a question to which all children have sought the answer. Peace is found in many unlikely quarters, yet all who seek it must find it in their own heart, for it lies within.'

'Can you give me no guidance then?' you ask.

'Help lies in many guises,' he answers, 'but if you have courage, look now within this globe, and maybe your quest will be achieved, and your hope for guidance be well founded.'

One of the other beings steps forwards and passes to him a large globe of crystal. He bids you sit, and places the globe on the ground in front of you, directing you to look into its depths. You find your eyes drawn to the swirls of many-patterned light within, until you cannot look away.

Suddenly the swirling pattens disappear, as if a curatin has been drawn, and you see a great circle of fourteen thrones, upon which sit beings of such radiant beauty and power that you watch, mesmerised. They seem to become aware of you at the same moment, and the tallest, clad in azure blue and holding a great sceptre of sapphire, says, 'Why come you here, child of the followers?'

You find yourself answering, 'I come to seek peace.'

The fourteen great beings laugh, yet it is kindly laughter, and he who is clad in azure continues, 'Then come, child, learn as much as you are able of peace.'

Each of the fourteen, beginning with him, gazes into your eyes, and in your mind you hear each tell of how peace is to be found.

(*Pause* . . .)

After what seems the passing of ages, the vision fades and again you see the swirling patterns of light, until they also fade into the crystal. You become aware once more of your surroundings and realise that you have been subtly changed by the vision in the crystal.

The golden-haired shining one again looks at you: 'Great honour has been shown to you, greater than you know, child of the followers; yet friend of the first-born must you be or the sight would not have been shown you. We would also tell you that peace is that brought by security. For the fences, be they of rock or of swords, may also allow peace to blossom as the flowers of delight within the garden of dreams.

'We must leave you now, child of the second-born. Maybe it will be our fate to meet again. If it is not, then fare you well in your world and use well the gifts of the Powers and the first-born, for they are not given lightly, or to many of your race.'

'But how will I find this place again? There is so much that I want to know.'

He smiles again: 'Clues there are, for those who look, for there are still some who hold us in thought. Seek for the stars that shine within the outer lands, for there may you find the entry again, if that is your destiny. Remember, it is said that understanding comes only with work!'

He bows and then he and his companions, taking the wondous crystal globe, turn and walk away down the path. As the sound of their footsteps fades, the stars too seem to pale and the glimmering path disappears.

You awaken and find yourself lying in the soft bracken of the moor, the memory of your dream and all you have been told of peace still vibrant and sharp within your mind. You rise, refreshed, and begin to walk on across the moor in the moonlight, looking in vain to see the cottage, but perhaps it too was part of your dream, for, strain your eyes as you will, you cannot see it.

MICHAEL BEECHEY

CHAPTER FIVE

INVOCATIONS
(Seeking Peace in its Many Forms)

*At death . . . [we are] separated from all that is not God . . . What
remains is the invocation alone.*
AL-GHAZALI

When we petition for something, whom do we invoke? In each
land, each tradition, each spiritual path, there are aspects of deity
which posses a unique link with peace. In the 'Litany of the Gods'
included in this chapter (see p. 171), I have tried to recall as many
as possible from around the world. The reader may well know of
others, and should add these or substitute them as appropriate.
Among the other pieces in this section there are invocations from
cultures as different as Egyptian, Celtic and Greek, as well as
modern invocations specially written for this book.

Invocation is like prayer, except that it draws upon the very
essence of deity or spirit. It is often no more than the uttering,
aloud, of the Holy Name, whatever that may be. Appealing to this
name can transform the condition of those who offer the
invocation: doors open before their eyes, their dreams are
replenished, inspiration dawns within them. In the words of
Richard of Saint-Victor: 'This is the invocation of the Name; this
is the possession of salvation . . . the union of the Word with the
soul in which every man is saved. For with such light no one can
be blind, with such power no one can be weak, with such salvation
none can perish.'

Sometimes we may be called upon to invoke the name of deity
in order to curb our desires. Thus in the 'Hymn to Ares' on p. 168,
the Greek god invoked is that of war: he is petitioned to restrain
the savagery which exists in the blood of humanity, and to look
with kindness upon those who are only too eager to take up the
weapons of war.

Whomever you invoke, remember to do so with serious intent.
You *will* be heard, and to seek answers for frivolous reasons, or
out of the simple fascination of calling upon strange gods, is to
bring a different kind of response. With wisdom and with the
empowering strength of the spirit, you may indeed invoke peace in
any one its many and wondrous forms, or as deity itself, however
you choose to view it.

A Prayer for Peace

Munificent queen of the gods O lady Hermouthis
Good Fortune almighty Isis whose names are great
Loftiest Deo you initiate all life
You concerned yourself with every activity
So that you could grant life and order to all
And you introduced laws for fairness to begin
And you gave skills to dignify our lives

You disclosed the natural burgeoning of all fruits
Your grace connects the sky and the whole earth
The breath of winds and the sweet light of the Sun
Your power inundates each stream of the Nile
At the rising of Sirius when water flows greedily
Over all the land to renew endless fecundity
As many humans as inhabit the limitless earth
Thracians or Greeks or people from other lands
So many give reverence to your beautiful name
Uttered by native tongues in each respective country

The Syrians call you Astarte-Artemis-Nanaia
And the Lycian races term you their lady Leto
The men of Thrace too call you the Mother Goddess
To the Greeks you are great-throned Hera and Aphrodite
And goodly Hestia and Rhea and Demeter too
In Egypt you are Thiouis for you are unique
Among all the goddesses whom different races name

O Queen I shall sing unceasingly of your mighty power
Undying Saviour greatest Isis of many names
You shield from battle both cities and all their inhabitants
Their women and possessions and their whole families
And all who are held in the prison of destiny and death
All who suffer great anguish and sleeplessness
And men who wander over foreign lands
And all who sail the ocean during great storms
When men are drowned and ships are shattered
You rescue each one who calls on you to be present

Hear my invocation O you whose name is so powerful
Be receptive to me and make all my suffering cease

ISIDORUS, *Hymn to Isis*,
trans. T. du Quesne

The Great Invocation

From the point of Light within the Mind of God
Let Light stream forth into the minds of men.
Let Light descend on Earth.

From the point of Love within the Heart of God
Let Love stream forth into the hearts of men.
May Christ* return to Earth.

From the Centre where the Will of God is known
Let Purpose guide the little wills of men –
The Purpose which the Masters know and serve.

From the Centre which we call the race of men
Let the Plan of Love and Light work out.
And may it seal the door where evil dwells.

Let Light and Love and Power restore the Plan on Earth.

ALICE A. BAILEY

*Many religions believe in a World Teacher, knowing him under such names as the
Lord Maitreya, the Imam Mahdi and the Messiah, and these terms are used in some
of the Hindu, Muslim, Buddhist and Jewish versions of 'The Great Invocation'.

*Invocation of the Angels of the Spheres and the Prince of Peace
for the Healing of the World*

The Earth is surrounded by loving and helpful spiritual intelli-
gences. We have but to realise their presence and call upon them
in faith to invoke their aid. Their presence, and their beneficient
influence, is always there, but this is increased a hundredfold if we
consciously realise it, and a thousandfold if we take time to help
actively in their mediation.

The way to do this is to reconstruct what C. S. Lewis called 'the
discarded image'. It is the vision of crystalline heavenly spheres
encircling the Earth. The image was discarded and forgotten when
material technology persuaded us that the physical universe was
constructed to another pattern, and so we lost our faith in the old
vision, but it is a model that still holds good in the spiritual worlds.

Be still within your room and form a dedicated centre. If there
is a group of you, sit in a circle around a candle or sanctuary light.
If you are alone, or if there are only two or three of you, imagine
you form part of a circle of like-minded souls who seek to aid you
in your work. It does not matter if you do not recognise your
invisible co-workers. Simply be aware of them in faith.

Become conscious of the world of nature outside your room: of
the trees, the plants, the flowers, the small animals, and the
elemental beings that organise their forces. Be aware, if you will,
of the great being of the Earth, Gaia herself, within her body of
earth and sea.

Be aware of her breathing, of the air enclosing the surface of the
Earth; the movement of the winds across the landscapes and the
oceans; the rise of water into the air through the warmth of the
Sun, and its precipitation again as dew, rain or snow. See the clouds
in the skies as changing expressions upon the face of nature.

And at the limits of the atmosphere see an encircling sphere of
protective light. This has sometimes been called a ring of inner fire.
It is the spiritual counterpart of what is called the ozone layer. It
withholds and protects the beings of the Earth in many unsuspected
ways.

Now imagine a sphere of crystal whose extent about the Earth
is as high as the Moon. You may imagine the figure of the Moon
upon its sphere, if you will, but there is no need to visualise more.
Simply be aware that the crystal sphere itself represents the tuned
consciousness of an order of angels that beams down strength and

constancy to humankind and all that live and move and have their being upon the planet.

There is no need to dwell long in this realisation once the initial effort is made. Extend your visualising powers to another crystal sphere whose bounds extend to the distance of Mercury. Be aware of this as the focussed consciousness of angels of intelligence and communication, bringing intellectual light to the denizens of the Earth below.

Now extend your vision to another crystal sphere, one that coincides with the orbit of Venus. It represents and radiates love and beauty to all below.

Pass on to visualise a further sphere, this one radiant with the Sun's light and as high as the Sun. It beams down, like the rays of the Sun, health, harmony, light and life-giving power to the Earth within its care.

Next see a crystalline sphere that coincides with the orbit of Mars, the focus for angelic beings of truth and right and justice.

Beyond this one, visualise the sphere that corresponds to the orbit of Jupiter and mediates the angelic influence of order and benign rulership.

And then imagine the crystal sphere that has at its limits far-off Saturn, and mediates the principles of organisation in form and the upholding of the necessary laws of nature.

Beyond this sphere is one that has engraved upon it, as on a crystal decanter, all the stars of the heavens visible to the human eye from Earth. These are the star angels whose influences pour in from the constellations. Not only those of the zodiac but of the other great asterisms such as the Pleiades and the Great Bear, and brilliant individual stars such as Sirius, Polaris, Regulus, or Vega, that beam down a plethora of spiritual inflences that are necessary for the well-being of the Earth.

And then beyond this is the outermost sphere of all, of complete clarity. It is the sphere of the holy angels themselves, sometimes called the Primum Mobile, that keeps all the cycles of being moving, be they cycles of time or cycles of space, of birth and growth and death, of individuals or of nations. And if you listen carefully, you may hear the angels singing; it is what has sometimes been called the harmony of the spheres – not only the harmony of the working of a beautiful organism, but also a paeon of praise for the Creative Spirit beyond who made it.

Our consciousness is not capable of penetrating beyond the outer sphere, even in symbolic vision. But a reflection of what lies beyond can come to our awareness. As an expression in sight and substance of the harmony of the spheres, see a holy rain begin to fall. It is as delicate as newly forming dew, like the lightest of light mists. And it falls gently but inexorably through all the spheres. See it pass through each and every one until it falls upon the Earth outside your room and brings a freshness and a new-washed feeling to all that is within.

And as you become aware of this you may see, in your midst, at the centre of your circle (which is also the centre of all the crystal spheres, and whose ultimate circumference is beyond them all in the Uncreate Reality), a growing radiance. You may see, or be otherwise aware of, no more than a sense of love and light, although many have seen standing in the centre a child, the Son of Light, the Ever-living Young One, radiating peace and seeking personal and individual contact with each and every one, head to head, heart to heart, and feet to feet, as signifying the Way.

If you can, be aware of and reciprocate this contact, and seek to mediate it to the world, so that it penetrates all humanity, and influences the actions of your own small life. Now let the vision fade, and return your attention back to the world of your present duties and desires.

GARETH KNIGHT

The Song of Long Life

I invoke the seven daughters of the sea
Who fashion the threads of the sons of long life.
May three deaths be taken from me!
May seven waves of good fortune be dealt to me!
May no evil spirits harm me on my circuit!
In flashing corslet without hindrance!
May my fame not perish!
May old age come to me, may death not come to me till I am old!

I invoke Senach of the seven periods of time.
Whom fairy women have reared on the breasts of plenty.
May my seven candles not be extinguished!
I am an indestructible stronghold.
I am an unshaken rock.
I am a precious stone.
I am the luck of the week.
May I live a hundred times a hundred years.
Each hundred of them apart!
I summon their boons to me.
May the grace of the Holy Spirit be upon me!

Fifth-century Irish,
trans. Kuno Meyer

Let the Forces of Light bring illumination to all mankind.
Let the Spirit of Peace be spread abroad.
May men of goodwill everywhere meet in a spirit of co-operation.
May forgiveness on the part of all men be the keynote at this time.
Let power attend the efforts of the Great Ones.
So let it be and help us to do our part.

ALICE A. BAILEY

Earth Spirit Invocation

(*Used as an invocation across Britain to Gaia in June 1985*)

Song to the Gnomes and to Gaia

Earth of Earth, from sweet-scented gardens and forest floors you bring forth life from death.

Deep within you are the secrets of healing and growth.

Earthly Mother, nuture us and help us to respect your bountiful gifts.

Song to the Sylphs

Air of Earth, your delicate blanket shelters all Earth's beings from the raw energies of space.

With your fresh breezes you herald the changes within Nature's cycle.

You are the medium of vibration and the breath of life.

Song to the Undines

Water of Earth, you are the soft Summer rain, the fathomless sea.

From our very beginnings you protect and support us with your hidden strength.

Heal us with your crystal springs and gently cleanse the land with your mighty rivers.

Song to the Salamanders

Fire of Earth, you bring warmth and comfort to our lives.

You are the rising force of Springtide, giving joy to all creatures.

You are the transformer, the purifier, and the gift of light.

HELENE HESS and KEN MILLS

Advent Peace Psalm

(Based on Chapter 31 of the Tao Te Ching)

O Prince of Peace,
    whose advent we seek in our lives,
    come this day and show us
    how to beat our swords into plowshares,
    tools of life instead of instruments of fear.

May your love strip us naked
    of all weapons and strategies of conquest,
    which are not the tools of lovers,
    wise ones and God's children.

Let us not lust for power
    but rather strive for the insight
    to be guided on the Way of Peace.

Let us not yearn for a victory
    that requires a sister's sorrow
    or a brother's shamefaced defeat.
With tears, black suits and dresses
    and tolling funeral bells,
    let us attend life's victory parties
    that are won at such a cost.

Let us be Advent adventurers and peacemakers,
    hammering swords into shovels,
    filling holes and leveling peaks.
Let us be disarmed and vulnerable,
    for only through such open hands and hearts
    can Emmanuel come.

EDWARD HAYS

Hymn to Ares

Ares, exceeding in strength, chariot-rider, golden-helmed, doughty in heart, shield-bearer, Saviour of cities, harnessed in bronze, strong of arm, unwearying, mighty with the spear, O defence of Olympus, father of warlike Victory, ally of Themis, stern governor of the rebellious, leader of righteous men, sceptred King of manliness, who whirl your fiery sphere among the planets in their sevenfold courses through the aether wherein your blazing steeds ever bear you above the third firmament of heaven; hear me, helper of men, giver of dauntless youth! Shed down a kindly ray from above upon my life, and strength of war, that I may be able to drive away bitter cowardice from my head and crush down the deceitful impulses of my soul. Restrain also the keen fury of my heart which provokes me to tread the ways of blood-curdling strife. Rather, O blessed one, give you me boldness to abide within the harmless laws of peace, avoiding strife and hatred and the violent fiends of death.

HESIOD

Let the Lords of Liberation issue forth.
Let Them bring succour to the sons of men.
Let the Rider from the secret Place come forth,
And coming, save.
Come forth, O Mighty One.

Let the souls of men awaken to the Light,
And may they stand with massed intent.
Let the fiat of the Lord go forth:
The end of woe has come!
Come forth, O Mighty One.
The hour of service of the Saving Force has now arrived.
Let is be spread abroad, O Mighty One.

Let Light and Love and Power and Death
Fulfil the purpose of the Coming One.
The Will to save is here,
The Love to carry forth the work is widely spread abroad.
The Active Aid of all who know the truth is also here.
Come forth, O Mighty One, and blend these three.
Construct a great defending wall.
The rule of evil *now* must end.

ALICE A. BAILEY

The Glastonbury Invocation

There is a source of Love which is the Heart of All Life
Let that Love flow
Source to Earth – Heart to Heart

There is a source of Light which is the Mind of All Life
Let that Light flow
Source to Earth – Mind to Mind

There is a source of Power which is the Purpose of All Life
Let that Power flow
Source to Earth – Purpose to Purpose

We are that Love
We are that Light
We are that Power

Peace and Healing on Earth

WILLIAM BLOOM

Litany of the Gods

From the darkness of war:	*Baldur protect us.*
From the destruction of war:	*Iris protect us.*
From the hatred of war:	*Quetzalcoatle protect us.*
From the terror of war:	*Mary protect us.*
From the horror of war:	*Enkidu protect us.*
From the separations of war:	*Sophia protect us.*
From the aftermath of war:	*Herne protect us.*
From the greed of war:	*Kuan Yin protect us.*
From the strife of war:	*Tammuz protect us.*
From the dread of war:	*Irene protect us.*
From the magnitude of war:	*El protect us.*
From the evils of war:	*Shekinah protect us.*
From the tortures of war:	*Deganawida protect us.*
From the devices of war:	*Avalokitesvara protect us.*

And may the People of Peace, the Faery Kind, the Lordly Ones, the Peacemakers, the Dwellers in Avalon, and all the species, animal, vegetable and mineral; all things that fly, crawl, swim and run upon the face of the Earth, our Mother; trees and flowers, vines and fruit, grain and herb, all things that grow; the air and the water, the earth and the fire – may they each and every one in their own unique way add their strengths, their qualities and abilities to ours. So that, in days to come, war may become a memory, and peace spread its wings across the world and in our hearts.

JOHN MATTHEWS

O Being of life!
O Being of peace!
O Being of time!
O Being of eternity!
O Being of eternity!

Keep me in good means,
Keep me in good intent,
Keep me in good estate,
Better than I know to ask,
Better than I know to ask!

Shepherd me this day,
Relieve my distress,
Enfold me this night,
Pour upon me Thy grace,
Pour upon me Thy grace!

Guard for me my speech,
Strengthen for me my love,
Illume for me the stream,
Succour Thou me in death,
Succour Thou me in death!

Traditional Gaelic

Petition to Makataeshigun

Patron of the deep
Patron of the dark
Patron of the night
Patron of the arcane
Patron of the hidden.
Forbear!
Stay far
From our sleep
From our minds
From our hearts
From our spirits.
Let our spirits wander
From depth to depth
From breadth to breadth,
Inward and outward
Within their beings,
In quiet for peace.

Ojibway petition to Makataeshigun,
Spirit of the Underworld

Go in Peace, Come in Peace

I shall sing praises now that the time of the singing of birds has come, and I shall answer in song: go in peace, rain. I shall look at the deeds of my God, so pleasant in their season, and sweetly say: come in peace, dew.

The rains are over and gone, the winter is past; everything is created with beauty: go in peace, rain.

The mandrakes give forth their perfume in the lovers' garden; sorrows are past: come in peace, dew.

The earth is crowned with new grain and wine, and every creature cries: go in peace, rain!

Traditional Hebrew

Invocation of Bran the Blessed

Great Bran, whose noble head sang for his followers for years unnumbered upon the Island of Gwales in Caer Siddi, you who were a bridge to your people, and who gave shape and purpose to the acts of those who followed you, I ask that you grant us the light of your blessing and that you guide our footsteps on the paths of peacefulness.

JOHN MATTHEWS

Invocation of the Shaper of All Things

O Shaper of All, who in the beginning gave form to all things, who took the stuff of matter and gave it life, do not take from us the light that was born in your dream. Come, be with us now, in this time of conflict and terror; guide our steps and make us one with your essence, which is of all things and all species, and which is one, for ever, with all Creation. Be with us now and at all times, and give us the freedom to choose life before death, hope before despair, truth before illusion, until we come into your presence – at which time let us be able to stand before you and address you with honour.

Anon.

An Invocation to the Goddess

From Ancient stillness you came,
Treading the path of vision, you walked the first directions.
Your moving beauty sparked into being the wind behind you.
Then you saw your other self. Pure Light. He in his beauty saw
    you. Pure Joy.
In your ecstasy for one another all things came into being.

As he touched and named each thing it moved with your vision
    and your form.
The universe hummed and sang in an eternity of oneness.
Then the first thought of 'I'-ness came and turned into duality.
All began to spin, he claimed the named ones and you cried out in
    your pangs of birth, of death and the dark ones.
Eternity became time, Creation became conscious of itself.

You wove the colours of his energy into a myriad of fragments.
You both danced the eternal dance of Light and Dark, of Ying and
    Yang, of love and hate, of Sorrow and Joy.
Spinning in space, ever creating, ever becoming and ever dying.
Waiting for the created to unfold your vision.
Then with a crack your mantle moved revealing the darkness
    beneath.
You created fear, he named it, you gave beauty a dark face, he
    scorned it.

Then out of Creation's darkness came the stirrings of desire, the
    search for Light and the beauty of Joy.
Eternity seeking itself. The gift of your circles girdled and adorned
    his waist.
The embrace of his desire and compassion encircled your heart of
    fire, of sorrow and understanding.
Then we will find you in stillness, and both of you in oneness.
Deep Peace will come, creating unity for ever in Joy and Light.

HELENE HESS

O Hidden Life! vibrant in every atom;
O Hidden Light! shining in every creature;
O Hidden Love! embracing all in Oneness;
May each who feels himself as one with Thee,
Know he is also one with every other.

ANNIE BESANT

CHAPTER SIX
GLEANINGS
(From the Dreams of Men and Women in Search of Peace)

Wisdom is better than weapons of war.

Ecclesiastes, 9:18

Throughout this book we have encountered the wisdom of great minds and souls in love with the idea of peace in all its manifestations. We have asked the question 'What is peace?' and have found many answers. We have sought, and found, ways in which we, as individuals living at the end of the twentieth century, may take part in the worldwide movement in search of peace. We have seen, also, that many who work for this movement – which has many names, many identities – remain unknown, working quietly in their own homes before shrines to peace, which they have made with their own hands.

In this last section we return to some of those whose works we have already learned from, as well as encountering new voices, and look in greater depth at what they have to say. As before, the range is wide: here are wise words and thoughts from the Chinese Book of Wisdom, the *I Ching*; from men and women of God; from those who continue to fight for the rights of people and for the Earth herself. There is a story from the Iroquois tradition of the Peacemaker; a passage on the Greek goddess Aphrodite; and, to end the book, words from one of the great peacemakers of our time, Mikhail Gorbachev. Indeed, as I write, Communism, for so long perceived as a threatening monster, is falling in the land which gave it form and substance.

This must surely be seen as one sign of an era of peace to come. Doubtless there will be setbacks, but it seems, at last, that the voices of sanity are beginning to be heard, and that we may one day see the paths to peace come together to form a great highway which all may walk.

Many people of peace have been persecuted through the centuries. I believe that the time of persecution has passed. The energies of the people are now being directed in search of ways to save Mother Earth. The founder of Haudenosaunee government, whom we call the Peacemaker, intended that there be social justice in the world. No man was to be more privileged than any other man. All were to be accorded respect. A healthy human mind respects the gifts of life – all nature gives life . . . Even as we enter a time of increasing potential for peace among the major powers, military expenditures remain grotesquely high. The purpose of these high military budgets must be the anticipation of violence. As a mother I demand that our sons not be raised to die in war. War is irrational, its causes suspect. If we are to live on this planet we must eliminate warfare, which is harmful to all living things.

AUDREY SHENANDOAH,
Onondaga Clan Mother

True peace can descend only if we depart from a society based on violence in which one forces his own will on the other. We must reunite ourselves spiritually with our brothers and sisters, and with all our 'relatives', the creatures of nature; we must let the Eternal Spirit rule on the earth. The Whole needs the vision of every individual entity, be it stone, plant, animal or human. The concern for all living things will then far surpass self-interest, and will bring greater happiness than ever before possible. Then all things will enjoy lasting harmony.

The Essence of Hopi Prophecy

The earth can no longer be healed on a physical level. Only a spiritual healing can change the course of the probable futures of mankind.

TOM BROWN, jun.

If warfare must continue, let us at least try to humanise it. Love may never rule in the city of man, but education could teach us that we need not kill one another in order to establish an identity.

SAM KEEN

The universe is a Unity, an interacting and genetically related community of beings bound together in an inseparable relationship in space and time. The Unity of the planet earth is especially clear; each being of the planet is profoundly implicated in the existence and functioning of every other being of the planet.

THOMAS BERRY

Peace begins in our own hearts in our willingness to skilfully state what we want with and from our family, friends, and co-workers. Through skilful communication we develop pathways of resolution so that all feel themselves respected in the circle of life. So just as the apparent conflict imitates the dynamic of family abuse, so too does the individual resolution to speak truth, to call for what is beneficial and to support communication and negotiation, create the ability for all to see that this is but one planet, one atmosphere that we share and that if one person on one side of the world is harmed, we all suffer. So it is the wise people who apply their citizenship responsibly as a voice for peace and resolution.

VEN. UGVWIYUHI DHYANI YWAHOO

Resolving interior conflicts that drive the cycle of war is imperative in the nuclear age. If wars arise out of weakness, humankind must travel beyond weakness to create harmony and peace.

MICHAEL TOMS

Roots have spread out from the Tree of the Great Peace . . . and the name of these roots is the Great White Roots of Peace. If any man of any nation outside of the Five Nations shall show a desire to obey the laws of the Great Peace . . . they may trace the roots to their source . . . and they shall be welcomed to take shelter beneath the Tree of the Long Leaves.

DEGANAWIDAH, Iroquois Peacemaker

The Traveller has reached the end of the journey! . . . In the light of his vision he has found his freedom: his thoughts are peace, his words are peace and his work is peace.

Dhammapada, vv. 90 and 96

The quality of calm derives from the divine Peace, which is made of Bliss, of infinite Beauty; beauty everywhere and always has at its root an aspect of calm, of equilibrium of possibilities; that is, it has an aspect of limitlessness and of happiness . . . Beauty bears within itself every element of happiness, whence its character of peace, plenitude, satisfaction; now beauty is in our very being, we live by its substance.

FRITHJOF SCHUON

Love and serve all humanity. Help everyone. Be happy. Be courteous. Be a dynamo of irrepressible joy. Recognise God and goodness in every face. There is no saint without a past and no sinner without a future. Praise everyone. If you cannot praise someone, let him go out of your life. Be original. Be inventive. Be courageous. Take courage again and again. Do not imitate. Be strong. Be upright. Think with your own head. Be yourself. Do not lean on the crutches of others. All perfection and every divine virtue are hidden within you – reveal them to the world. Wisdom too is already within you – let it strike forth. Let the Lord's grace make you free. Let your life be that of the rose – in silence it speaks the silence of fragrance.

BABAJI

Jonah and the Whale

(Scripture: the Book of Jonah, particularly 1:17)

We give picture books of Jonah and the Whale to our children. The story of Jonah shows that God can deliver us from the monsters that can eat us – and that is comforting.

When we read the scripture of Jonah for ourselves, we learn that God's love for his creation is infinitely greater than our own prejudices – and that is challenging.

But the story of Jonah was also a prophecy of the Messiah that was to come. Jonah's three days in the belly of the whale prefigures Christ's death and resurrection. The depiction of Hell in medieval manuscripts and cathedral carvings show Hell's mouth framed with great teeth. Even our expression 'snatched from the jaws of death' shows that the metaphor still has vividness.

We read the scripture of Jonah and give thanks that our Lord who delivered Jonah from the whale has the power to deliver us from despair in this life and through Jesus Christ from death itself – and this comforts us.

> I called to the Lord, out of my distress, and he answered me; out of the belly of death I cried, and thou didst hear my voice . . . Deliverance belongs to the Lord. (Jonah 2:2, 9)

MILDRED LEAKE DAY

We must learn much more about the pacifist tradition, the roots of non-violence and the struggle for freedom of conscience. And as a woman I must reiterate that especially my sisters must demand that the psychological, physical and economic violence perpetrated by men against women be recognized and ended and that social institutions be changed so as to no longer reflect the pattern of dominance and submission. We must turn towards encouraging a more human, loving standard of behaviour instead of relationships steeped in aggression, competition, exploitation. We women are so intimately close to our oppressors and this sometimes has made me pessimistic. We must explore new forms of relating.

The feminist vision, which is also an ecological one, abandons the concept of naming enemies and adopts the concept familiar to the non-violent tradition: naming behaviour that is oppressive, naming abuse of power that is held unfairly and must be destroyed, but naming *no person*, one whom we are willing to destroy. Barbara Dening has written: 'If we can destroy a man's power to be violent, there is no need of course to destroy the man himself. And if the same man who behaves in one sense as an oppressor, is in another sense our comrade, there is no need to fear that we have lost our political minds or souls when we treat him as a *person* divided from us and from himself in just this way.' We must always judge the social role and see behind that role the human being.

PETRA KELLY

While he is at his destination, as long as he does not return, the seeker is called 'one who stops' (*waqif*). Those who stop include the ones who are absorbed in that station, as for instance Abu-'Iqal and others. In it [God] takes them and in it they are resurrected. The classification *waqif* also includes the ones who are sent back (*mardudun*). These are more perfect than the absorbed ones (*mustahlikun*), if they equal each other in station. If [one seeker] is absorbed in a higher station than that from which [another seeker] returns, then we do not say that the returned one is higher. The condition for drawing a comparison is the mutual resemblance of the two. If that condition is met, then the returned one lives, having descended from the station of the absorbed one, so that he reaches the degree of the absorbed one and surpasses him in drawing near, surpasses him in coming down, and excels him in development and reception of knowledge.

IBN 'ARABI

We live in a time of prophets and visionaries, and there is constant speculation in the sphere of mysteries. To those to whom it is given can come the power to see more clearly, and so be able to guide others towards good, having themselves understood evil. The powers of saints and holy men and women in all ages are achieved by their understanding of their own negative energies, by learning to control them through the practice of a regular discipline, and by then harnessing that transformed energy to the service of a will that inclines towards the positive. Such powers alone can rise to combat the ever-resurgent powers of evil to which the world is always subject. If every individual would have first the courage to seek the truth within himself that leads to personal inner peace, then there would be a possibility of spreading that peace from the individual to the multitude.

HOWARD BLAKE

'*Peace is the Tranquillity of Order*'

– Thomas Aquinas

Honour is peace, the peace which does accord
Alone, with God's glad word:
'*My peace I send you, and I send a sword.*'

The unprecedented prosperity of the nineteenth century that led English Empire-builders to imagine themselves the undisputed guides and guardians of mankind exploded in a flash under the bombshell of World War I. Since then, as this twentieth century has run its course, has the world ever witnessed so many millions of human beings with arms uplifted to kill, so many innocent people drenched in blood? Yet the century is drawing to a close with a nuclear threat of unimaginable disaster. World history has reached a point when action becomes the primary duty of every citizen who would refuse to sit at ease admiring the rippling foam that conceals the billow of the earthquake beneath, but would rise at once to defend his own and his neighbour's household from clearly discerned destruction. Each must speak out clearly, 'for a good word then is a good deed'.

During the last decade, a bow has been set in the cloud and opened up a new horizon of possible peace. The situation calls urgently for a Hildebrand able to arouse the conscience of the world, an umpire disencumbered of personal interests, possessed by his position of knowledge and statesmanship, and given the support of a worldwide confederation of nations necessary to punish any who should refuse to acknowledge his authority.

Who shall be nominated?

SISTER FELICITAS CORRIGAN, OSB

11. T'ai / Peace

above K'UN   THE RECEPTIVE, EARTH
below CH'IEN   THE CREATIVE, HEAVEN

The Receptive, which moves downward, stands above; the Creative, which moves upward, is below. Hence their influences meet and are in harmony, so that all living things bloom and prosper. This hexagram belongs to the first month (February–March), at which time the forces of nature prepare the new spring.

THE JUDGMENT

PEACE. The small departs,
The great approaches.
Good fortune. Success.

This hexagram denotes a time in nature when heaven seems to be on earth. Heaven has placed itself beneath the earth, and so their powers unite in deep harmony. Then peace and blessing descend upon all living things.

In the world of man it is a time of social harmony; those in high places show favor to the lowly, and the lowly and inferior in their turn are well disposed toward the highly placed. There is an end to all feuds.

Inside, at the center, in the key position, is the light principle; the dark principle is outside. Thus the light has a powerful influence, while the dark is submissive. In this way each receives its due. When the good elements of society occupy a central position and are in control, the evil elements come under their influence and change for the better. When the spirit of heaven rules in man, his animal nature also comes under its influence and takes its appropriate place.

The individual lines enter the hexagram from below and leave it again at the top. Here the small, weak, and evil elements are about to take their departure, while the great, strong, and good elements are moving up. This brings good fortune and success.

Heaven and earth unite: the image of PEACE.
Thus the ruler
Divides and completes the course of heaven and earth;
He furthers and regulates the gifts of heaven and earth,
And so aids the people.

Heaven and earth are in contact and combine their influences, producing a time of universal flowering and prosperity. This stream of energy must be regulated by the ruler of men. It is done by a process of division. Thus men divide the uniform flow of time into the seasons, according to the succession of natural phenomena, and mark off infinite space by the points of the compass. In this way nature in its overwhelming profusion of phenomena is bounded and controlled. On the other hand, nature must be furthered in her productiveness. This is done by adjusting the products to the right time and the right place, which increases the natural yield. This controlling and furthering activity of man in his relation to nature is the work on nature that rewards him.

I Ching

The Roots of Peace

There was a dark time before the great Confederacy, when all the nations of the Iroquois were at war with each other, and the people were weak, and the Mahicans and the Adirondacks attacked and slew them at will. Then the Peace Maker came out of the west.

He came in a canoe made of glittering white stone which was very heavy, yet it did not sink, but flew swiftly over the water of the lake. He was a messenger from the Master of Life, who had revealed to his grandmother in a dream that a child would be born to her virgin daughter, and he would bring the good news of peace and power to the people, and that his name would be the Peace Maker. And so he was born, and grew, and came out of the west in his white stone canoe.

The first people he met were hunters, and he gave them the message to take back to their chiefs that the fighting must cease. And he went to the house of a woman, who fed him, and he gave her the message of peace and power in its three parts: justice, health, and law. And he told her there would be a longhouse, and a council of nations, and unity between them. The woman was glad and embraced the message, and the Peace Maker made her the mother of nations.

Then he continued eastward and came to the house of the Man Who Eats Humans, who had just put a kettle on the fire with the meat of a human body in it. The Peace Maker climbed to the roof and looked down the smoke hole, and his face was reflected in the water of the kettle. The Man Who Eats Humans saw the reflected face and was amazed, for it was his own face, and yet it was wise and noble.

'I didn't know that I was like that,' he said. 'This is not the face of a man who eats human flesh. I see it is not like me to do that, and I shall not do it anymore,' and he took the kettle outside and emptied it. Then the Peace Maker came to him and entered the house with him and gave him the message of peace and power, and the man embraced it. The Peace Maker went out and killed a deer and brought it back for their food. 'It is the meat of deer that men must eat,' he said, 'and their antlers placed on men's heads shall be the sign of authority,' and ever since that day the chiefs of the Five Nations have worn the horns of the deer.

The Peace Maker told the man that he was to be his messenger, and that he was to spread the news of the Great Peace and to convert the chiefs of the people. The hardest part of his task would be to convert a magician-chief of the Onondagas whose name was Atotarho, and who was so strong and cruel and evil that all men and animals feared him. His body was twisted seven times, and his hair was a mass of writhing snakes. For this reason, the Peace Maker gave the man who was to be his messenger the name of Hiawatha, He Who Combs, because he would prevail over Atotarho and comb the snakes from his hair.

The Peace Maker went among the people, and the first he converted to the Great Law were the Mohawks. Hiawatha went to begin his struggle with Atotarho, but Atotarho mocked him and put evil spells on all three of his daughters and on his wife, so that they died. Hiawatha was so overcome with grief that he could no longer bear the land of the Onondagas, and he went south and sat on the shore of the lake to mourn. He made strings of shells and sang songs of grief, begging for someone to come and make the shell strings into words of consolation. At last the Peace Maker came and listened, and he also made strings of shell and put them with Hiawatha's, and spoke words of consolation that are still used with the wampum strings by the people; and Hiawatha was freed from his grief.

After this, the Peace Maker and Hiawatha went to the Oneidas and the Cayugas and the Senecas and converted them all to the Great Law of Peace, and also all the chiefs of the Onondagas except Atotarho. The Peace Maker told him that he would be the chief of all the Council and the Keeper of the Council fire. Atotarho wished for this and for peace but asked where was the power. Then the Peace Maker called all the chiefs of all the nations, and they came together and were as one; and the Peace Maker said, 'Here is power.' Then Atotarho's mind was changed, and Hiawatha combed the snakes from his hair, and the seven twists came out of his body. The Peace Maker placed the antlers on his head and on the heads of the other chiefs and taught them the words of the law.

And he planted a pine tree, and called it the Tree of Peace; and four roots spread out, to the four directions. Then he uprooted the tree, and took all the weapons of war and threw them in the hole under the tree, and then he planted the tree again. In the topmost branches he placed an eagle, to watch and cry out if any evil approached the people.

Roots have spread out from the Tree of the Great Peace, one to the north, one to the east, one to the south, and one to the west. These are the Great White Roots, and their nature is Peace and Strength.

If any man or any nation shall obey the laws of the Great Peace . . . they may trace the roots to their source . . . and they shall be welcomed to take shelter beneath the Tree . . .

Traditional Iroquois

The pebbles in the mountain torrent, through the tearing movement of the water, roll and tumble against the rocks, but in that struggle they grow polished, and finally get fretted into powder, whereby their course is facilitated towards the fulfilment of their Destiny – absorption in the Ocean.

There are pebbles, however, which take refuge in the quiet backwaters of the stream, where they lie dormant and quiet, relieved from the stress and fury of the raging torrent, but they make no progress towards the Ocean, where alone they can attain to true peace and rest.

Who are the despised of the despised? They who do neither Good nor Evil; they who take refuge in the Negation of action; they who hope that they will obtain the Crown of Reward because they have neither known the Passion of Evil nor the Passion of Good!

The Chord of the Harp which cannot vibrate is a Chord which might as well not exist, as it contributes nothing to the Manifestation of the Divine Harmony. Than the stagnant Soul of a Man, more profitable to the Soul of Humanity is the individual Soul which vibrates to the intensity of Evil, for such vibration by its intensity engenders vibration in the opposite direction, the direction of Good, whereby the progress of the Soul of Humanity on the Path of Destiny is accelerated.

HAJI IBRAHIM OF KERBELA

After Ragnarok

The earth will rise again out of the water, fair and green. The eagle will fly over cataracts, swoop into the thunder and catch fish under crags. Corn will ripen in fields that were never sown.

Vidar and Vali will still be alive; they will survive the fire and the flood and make their way back to Idavoll, the shining plain where palaces once stood. Modi and Magni, sons of Thor, will join them there, and they will inherit their father's hammer, Mjollnir. And Baldur and Hod will come back from the world of the dead; it will not be long before they, too, tread the new green grass on Idavoll. Honir will be there as well, and he will hold the wand and foretell what is to come. The sons of Vili and Ve will make up the new number, the gods in heaven, home of the winds.

They will sit down in the sunlight and begin to talk. Turn by turn, they will call up such memories, memories such as are known to them alone. They will talk over many things that happened in the past, and the evil of Jormungand and the wolf Fenrir. And then, amongst the waving grass, they will find golden chessboards, treasures owned once by the Aesir, and gaze at them in wonder.

Traditional Norse,
retold by Kevin Crossley-Holland

Mir – a Mirror of Peace in the Sky

On August 6, 1981 the word MIR, meaning peace, was written in large letters across the sky, above Mt. Krizevak with its cross visible in the foreground. It was witnessed by thousands. It has also been seen several times since then, and is a beautiful manifestation of one of the Madonna's most important messages.

Also, painted on the sky as if it were a canvas, a star show has appeared occasionally. Ordinary stars, in their normal positions, have been seen revolving in the sky. As if that wasn't enough, these same stars alternately turned on and off, like strobe lights, for over an hour. This occurred on June 18, 1982 and June 19, 1982, the Feasts of the Sacred Heart and Immaculate Heart, respectively. It was observed again in 1984.

ANN MARIE HANCOCK

Remember that it is not only desire of office and of wealth that makes men abject and subservient to others, but also desire of peace and leisure and travel and learning. Regard for any external thing, whatever it be, makes you subservient to another . . . What, pray, is this peace of mind, which any one can hinder – I do not mean Caesar, or Caesar's friend, but a raven, a flute-player, a fever, countless other things? Nothing is so characteristic of peace of mind as that it is continuous and unhindered . . . There is but one way to peace of mind (keep this thought by you at dawn and in the day-time and at night) – to give up what is beyond your control, to count nothing your own, to surrender everything to heaven and fortune, to leave everything to be managed by those to whom Zeus has given control, and to devote yourself to one object only, that which is your own beyond all hindrance.

EPICTETUS

I live at the heart of a single, unique Element, the Center of the Universe, and present in each part of it: personal Love and cosmic Power.

To attain to Him and become merged into His life, I have before me the entire universe with its noble struggles, its impassioned quests, its myriad of souls to be healed and made perfect. I can and I must throw myself into the thick of human endeavor, and with no stopping for breath. For the more fully I play my part and the more I bring my efforts to bear on the whole surface of reality, the more also will I attain to Christ and cling close to him. God who is eternal Being-in-itself, is, one might say, ever in process of formations *for us*.

And God is also the heart of everything; so much so that the vast setting of the universe might be engulfed or wither away or be taken from me by death without my joy being diminished. Were creation's dust, which is vitalized by a halo of energy and glory, to be swept away, the substantial Reality wherein every perfection is incorruptibly contained and possessed would remain intact; the rays would be drawn back onto their Source and there I should still hold them all in a close embrace.

TEILHARD DE CHARDIN

Look at a stream flowing from its source to the Ocean; it is an unbroken current, it is a complete whole. Yet the mind can conceive it as made up of an infinite number of drops of water, each perfect in itself, having individual identity, being a complete whole. And the mind can conceive each individual drop of water influenced as to its identity, modified as to its character, by the nature of the current, its rapidity, its slowness, its stagnation, and being clean or unclean according to the quality of the soil and land which contains the current and influences its course.

Look now at the Stream of the Soul of Humanity. It is likewise an unbroken whole flowing from the Unity and returning to the Unity; and this stream is formed of the Souls of Men; the drops of water, each possessed of identity and individuality, and clean or unclean according to the nature of the current around them, and quality of the soil over which they pass and the influence exerted on them by the constraining land, the Phenomenal World through which the Stream of the Soul of Humanity passes and whose Law governs the progress of its flow.

HAJI IBRAHIM OF KERBELA

Aphrodite: Personification of Peace

The 'Homeric Hymn to Aphrodite' calls this sweet-smelling goddess of sensuality the 'lover of laughter', who dislikes three things only: warmongering, the murder of animals, and chastity. Greek myth provides a sophisticated comment on love's supremacy over war. Aphrodite's main lover is the god of war – Ares – said to be the most hated god on Olympus because of his addiction to violence. Her 'husband' is Hephaestus, the blacksmith god and armourer.

The war-god melts under her spells. Aphrodite/Venus does not turn her back on militarism, but faces its personification in Ares/Mars, seduces him – away from the battlefield and into her bed – making love, not war. While Hephaestus is obsessed by her beauty and possessed in her presence, she distracts him from spending time making arms or instruments of war. Libido invested in the economics of the industrial war machine – Hephaestus' realm – is reclaimed by Aphrodite and invested in concern for peaceful intimacy and tolerant relationships. She takes the closed fist and transforms it into a giving hand, teaching caress and embrace.

Aphrodite represents the vegetable-green heart of an aesthetic and erotic ecology, loving to a paradoxical death the reds of blood spilled in warring. She turns the political body of desire for control and power into an eroticised desire for peaceful community; and transforms narcissistic self-interest into a love for the world and its beauty.

ALAN BLEAKLEY

'Happiness in Tranquillity,' which, as already noted, is not separately developed in distinct compositions, but underlies all as a kind of drone over which they play. Its 'permanent state' is *sāma*, 'peace of mind,' which is characterized by 'tranquility, indifference to the objects of sense, and repose in the knowledge of *brahman*,' while the 'sentiment,' or *rasa*, by which the realization is flavored is the 'peaceful' (*śānta-rasa*) the experience of which is an effect simply of the harmonious composition of the work of art: what Joyce would have called its 'rhythm of beauty,' *consonantia*, its relation of part to part, of each part to the whole, and of the whole to each of its parts.

JOSEPH CAMPBELL

Thus saw I that God is our very Peace, and He is our sure Keeper when we are ourselves in unpeace, and He continually worketh to bring us into endless peace.

Full preciously our Lord keepeth us when it seemeth to us that we are near forsaken and cast away for our sin and because we have deserved it. And because of meekness that we get hereby, we are raised well-high in God's sight by His grace, with so great contrition, and also compassion, and true longing to God. Then they be suddenly delivered from sin and from pain, and taken up to bliss, and made even high saints.

By contrition we are made clean, by compassion we are made ready, and by true longing toward God we are made worthy. These are three means, as I understand, whereby that all souls come to heaven: that is to say, that have been sinners in earth and shall be saved: for by these three medicines it behoveth that every soul be healed. Though the soul be healed, his wounds are seen afore God – not as wounds but as worships. And so on the contrary-wise, as we be punished here with sorrow and penance, we shall be rewarded in heaven by the courteous love of our Lord God Almighty, who willeth that none that come there lose his travail in any degree. For he [be]holdeth sin as sorrow and pain to His lovers, to whom He assigneth no blame, for love. The meed that we shall receive shall be little, but it shall be high, glorious, and worshipful. And so shall shame be turned to worship and more joy.

But our courteous Lord willeth not that His servants despair, for often nor for grievous falling: for our falling hindereth not him to love us. Peace and love are ever in us, being and working; but we be not always in peace and in love. But he willeth that we take heed thus that He is Ground of all our whole life in love; and furthermore that He is our everlasting Keeper and mightily defendeth us against our enemies.

DAME JULIAN OF NORWICH

There lives no man on earth who may always have rest and peace without troubles and crosses, with whom things go always according to his will. There is always something to be suffered here, consider it as you will. Seek only that true peace of the heart, which none can take away from you, that you may overcome all adversity; the peace that breaks through all adversities and crosses, all oppression, suffering, misery, humiliation, and what more there may be of the like, so that a man may be joyful and patient therein. Now if a man were lovingly to give his whole diligence and might thereto, he could very soon come to know that true eternal peace which is God Himself, as far as it is possible to a creature; insomuch that his heart would remain ever unmoved among all things.

Theologia Germanica

My proposal is that the cosmology of peace is presently the basic issue. The human must be seen in its cosmological role just as the cosmos needs ⁻to be seen in its human manifestation. This cosmological context has never been more clear than it is now, when everything depends on a *creative resolution of our present antagonisms.* I refer to a *creative resolution of antagonism* rather than to *peace* in deference to the violent aspects of the cosmological process. Phenomenal existence itself seems to be a violent mode of being. Also, there is a general feeling of fullness bordering on decay that is easily associated with *peace.* Neither *violence* nor *peace* in this sense is in accord with the creative transformations through which the more splendid achievements of the universe have taken place. As the distinguished anthropologist A. L. Kroeber once indicated: The ideal situation for any individual or any culture is not exactly 'bovine placidity.' It is, rather, 'the highest state of tension that the organism can bear creatively.'

In this perspective the present question becomes not the question of conflict or peace, but how we can deal creatively with these enormous tensions that presently afflict our planet. As Teilhard suggests, we must go beyond the human into the universe itself and its mode of functioning. Until the human is understood as a dimension of the earth, we have no secure basis for understanding any aspect of the human. We can understand the human only through the earth. Beyond the earth, of course, is the universe and the curvature of space. This curve is reflected in the curvature of the earth and finally in that psychic curve whereby the entire universe reflects back on itself in human intelligence.

This binding curve that draws all things together simultaneously produces with the inner forces of matter that expansive tension whereby the universe and the earth continue on their creative course. Thus the curve is sufficiently closed to hold all things together while it is sufficiently open to continue its creative emergence into the future. This tenuous balance between collapse and explosion contains the larger mystery of that functional cosmology which provides our most profound understanding of our human situation, even if it does not bring it within reach of our rational processes.

In this context our discussion of peace might well be understood primarily in terms of the Peace of Earth. This is not simply *Pax Romana* or *Pax Humana,* but *Pax Gaia,* the Peace of Earth, from the ancient mythic name for the planet.

THOMAS BERRY

The Power of Love

Sometimes it happens that love is sweetly awoken in the soul and joyfully arises and moves in the heart of itself without us doing anything at all. And then the heart is so powerfully touched by love, so keenly drawn into love and so strongly seized by love, and so utterly mastered by love and so tenderly embraced by love that it entirely yields itself to love. And in this it experiences a great proximity to God, a spiritual radiance, a marvellous bliss, a noble freedom, an ecstatic sweetness, a great overpowering by the strength of love, and an overflowing abundance of immense delight. And then she feels that all her senses are sanctified by love and her will has become love, and that she is so deeply immersed and so engulfed in the abyss of love that she herself has turned entirely into love. Then the beauty of love has bedecked her, the power of love has devoured her, the sweetness of love has submerged her, the grandeur of love has consumed her, the nobility of love has enveloped her, the purity of love has adorned her, and the sublimity of love has drawn her upwards and so united herself with her that she always must be love and do nothing but the deeds of love.

BEATRICE OF NAZARETH

'Everyone Loves the Beautiful Death of Soldiers'

– Song of a Tibetan camp follower

The following short speech was delivered to the Tibetan Army by the nine-year-old Dalai Lama at the funeral of a young soldier killed during a border skirmish with the Chinese:

Every warrior goes into battle with a vision of peace.

Every man of peace goes to the temple to watch the gods war with the devils.

The most beautiful spirits ever to enter the heavens are the spirits of soliders rising from the battlefields.

We are terrified by soldiers when they live, but when they die we love the peace that settles on their faces.

My brave and troubled soldiers, do not expect us to love you while you live, but take consolation in knowing that we love your deaths far more than the deaths of priests whose pent-up rage breaks out upon their flesh when the spirit departs, turning their faces into hideous masks.

PIERRE DELATTRE

God to me is inner peace. When the mind is freed from the outer turmoils of the world, it becomes peaceful. In that peaceful state of mind, God's love can be experienced. Ultimately, this love has no explanation, but rather is a pure state of mind.

When I was six years old I started feeling trapped in the world. The sky and earth became a box for me and I began to feel closed inside. My mind had imprisoned itself – but projected a box in the outer world. In that agitated state of mind a strong desire to leave developed. But to leave what? After I knocked on several doors to find the answer, it came from inside: Leave all those things that disturb the peace. When the mind is in peace, that is internal existence – and that is God. That is why I use the term 'peace' to explain God. Peace is not a dual state but an ever-existing reality . . .

Ultimately, we are all capable of understanding this simple truth: Peace can indeed be found in this world – and God is peace. The more our minds are involved in the outer things of the world, the less we understand ourselves and the less we experience God . . .

I cultivated my inner peace and relationship with God by fighting within myself, by my inner succeses and defeats. This peace, or experience of God, now separates the two worlds for me; the outer world is still projected, but without the attachment that gives it a reality. An analogy would be a man who decides to sell his new car – the car can still be beautiful without belonging to him.

If we are to create a peaceful world in the future we must begin with the experience of inner peace, the experience of God. God is not somewhere else; we are God. We are God and we are in God. It's simply a matter of acceptance. Accept yourself, accept others, and accept the world. When you do, pain will still come, just like pleasure. Hate will come, just like love. And when both are accepted, unaffected by the peaceful mind – there will be peace on earth.

BABA HARI DASS

Liberation

Now as to the man who is free from desire.

He who is free from desire, whose desire finds fulfilment, since the Spirit is his desire, the powers of life leave him not. He becomes one with Brahman, the Spirit, and enters into the Spirit. There is a verse that says:

When all desires that cling to the heart disappear, then a mortal becomes immortal, and even in this life attains Liberation.

As the slough of a snake lies dead upon an ant-hill, even so the mortal body; but the incorporeal immortal Spirit is life and light and Eternity.
Concerning this are these verses:

I have found the small path known of old that stretches far away. By it the sages who know the Spirit arise to the regions of heaven and thence beyond to liberation.
It is adorned with white and blue, yellow and green and red. This is the path of the seers of Brahman, of those whose actions are pure and who have inner fire and light.

Into deep darkness fall those who follow action. Into deeper darkness fall those who follow knowledge.

There are worlds of no joy, regions of utter darkness. To those worlds go after death those who in their unwisdom have not wakened up to light.

When awake to the vision of the Atman, our own Self, when a man in truth can say: 'I am He', what desires could lead him to grieve in fever for the body?

He who in the mystery of life has found the Atman, the Spirit, and has awakened to his light, to him as creator belongs the world of the Spirit, for he is this world.

While we are here in this life we may reach the light of wisdom; and if we reach it not, how deep is the darkness. Those who see the light enter life eternal: those who live in darkness enter into sorrow.

When a man sees the Atman, the Self in him, God himself, the Lord of what was and of what shall be, he fears no more.

Before whom the years roll and all the days of the years, him the gods adore as the Light of all lights, as Life immortal;

In whom the five hosts of beings rest and the vastness of space, him I know as Atman immortal, him I know as eternal Brahman.

Those who know him who is the eye of the eye, the ear of the ear, the mind of the mind and the life of life, they know Brahman from the beginning of time.

'The Supreme Teaching',
from the *Upanishads*

Even as the unwise work selfishly in the bondage of selfish works, let the wise man work unselfishly for the good of all the world.

Let not the wise disturb the mind of the unwise in their selfish work. Let him, working with devotion, show them the joy of good work.

All actions take place in time by the interweaving of the forces of Nature; but the man lost in selfish delusion thinks that he himself is the actor.

But the man who knows the relation between the forces of Nature and actions, sees how some forces of Nature work upon other forces of Nature, and becomes not their slave.

Those who are under the delusion of the forces of Nature bind themselves to the work of these forces. Let not the wise man who sees the All disturb the unwise who sees not the All.

Offer to me all thy works and rest thy mind on the Supreme. Be free from vain hopes and selfish thoughts, and with inner peace fight thou thy fight.

Those who ever follow my doctrine and who have faith, and have a good will, find through pure work their freedom.

But those who follow not my doctrine, and who have illwill, are men blind to all wisdom, confused in mind: they are lost.

'Even a wise man acts under the impulse of his nature: all beings follow nature. Of what use is restraint?'

Hate and lust for things of nature have their roots in man's lower nature. Let him not fall under their power: they are the two enemies in his path.

And do thy duty, even if it be humble, rather than another's, even if it be great. To die in one's duty is life: to live in another's death.

Bhagavad Gita, III

Peace is now reduced to two meanings: the myth that, at least in economics, two and two will one day make five, or a truce and deadlock. Development is the name given to the expansion of this game, to the incorporation of more players and of their resources. Therefore, the monopoly of *pax economica* must be deadly; and there must be some peace other than the one linked to development. One can concede that *pax economica* is not without some positive value – bicycles have been invented and their components must circulate in markets different from those in which pepper was formerly traded. And peace among economic powers is at least as important as peace between the warlords of ancient times. But the monopoly of this elite peace must be questioned. To formulate this challenge seems to me the most fundamental task of peace research today.

IVAN ILLICH

Great are the dangers facing mankind. There are enough elements of confrontation, but the forces wishing and capable of stopping and overcoming that confrontation are growing in strength and scope before our very eyes.

Moving from suspicion and hostility to confidence, from a 'balance of fear' to a balance of reason and good will . . . This is the goal of our peace initiative and for this we shall continue tirelessly to work.

MIKHAIL GORBACHEV

SOURCES AND
ACKNOWLEDGEMENTS

The following is a list of sources, where known, for all the material quoted in this book, giving acknowledgement to copyright owners where applicable. When a piece has been taken from another work – in other words, when it has not been written specifically for this book – the original spelling and punctuation have been retained. The publishers would like to thank those copyright holders who have granted permission to reprint material in this book. In some instances it has proved difficult to trace copyright holders or provide a full bibliographic citation of sources, and apologies are tendered in advance to proprietors and publishers concerned. The publishers of this book will be glad to make good any omissions brought to their attention in future editions.

p. 11: Black Elk, *The Sacred Pipe: Black Elk's Account of the Seven Rites of the Oglala Sioux*, ed. Joseph Epes Brown (Penguin Books, London, 1971). Copyright © 1953 by the University of Oklahoma Press. Reprinted by permission of Oklahoma University Press

p. 13: Frithjof Schuon, *Spiritual Perspectives* (Perennial Books, London, 1970)
   Bishop Ignatius Brianchinov, *On the Prayer of Jesus*, trans. Father Lazarus (J. M. Watkins, London, 1965). Reprinted by permission of Element Books Ltd, Shaftesbury

p. 14: Angelus Silesius, *Pèlerus chérubinique (The Cherubic Wanderer)*, I.237 from *A Treasury of Traditional Wisdom*, ed. Whitall N. Perry (Allen & Unwin, London, 1971)

p. 15: Hermes Trismegistus, *Hermetica*, ed. and trans. Walter Scott (Clarendon Press, Oxford, 1924–36). Reprinted by permission of Oxford University Press

p. 16: Alice A. Bailey, 'The Mantram of Unification' from *Discipleship in the New Age* (The Lucis Press, London), Vol. II, pp. 146–7. Reprinted by permission of the Lucis Trust Ltd

p. 18: Prudence Jones, 'Prayer of the Great Goddess'. Reprinted by permission of the author
   Christine Worthington, 'Druid Prayer'. Reprinted by permission of the author

A Jewish child's prayer, 'Lord, may I sleep . . .' from *Forms of Prayer*, Vol. I, Daily and Sabbath Prayerbook (Reform Synagogues of Great Britain, London, 1977). Reprinted by permission

p. 19: Traditional Gaelic, 'Blessing of the Goddess Badb' from *Carmina Gadelica* by Alexander Carmichael (Scottish Academic Press, Edinburgh, 1971). Reprinted by permission of Scottish Academic Press Ltd
Alice A. Bailey, *Discipleship in the New Age* (The Lucis Press, London), Vol. II, p. 305. Reprinted by permission of the Lucis Trust.
Aristophanes, 'O thou that makest wars . . .' from *Two-Part Invention* by Madeline L'Engle (Harper & Row, New York, 1988)

p. 20: 'Prayer to Nārāyanī' from *Kali: The Feminine Force* by Ajit Mookerjee (Thames & Hudson, London, 1988). Reprinted by permission of the publishers

p. 21: Buddhist Prayer, 'Loving Kindness' from *Only One Earth* (United Nations Environmental Sabbath Day Project, New York, n.d.)

p. 22: 'Prayer to Rudra' from *The Rig Veda*, trans. Wendy Doniger O'Flaherty (Penguin Classics, London, 1981). Copyright © Wendy Doniger O'Flaherty, 1981. Reprinted by permission of Penguin Books Ltd

p. 23: Jamie Sams/Midnight Song, 'Prayer for the Children'. Reprinted by permission of the author

p. 24: *Atharva Veda*, XIX from *Earth Prayers*, ed. E. Roberts and E. Amidon (Harper Collins, New York, 1991). Copyright © 1991 by Elizabeth Roberts and E. Amidon. Reprinted by permission of Harper Collins Publishers
Traditional Gaelic, 'Petition' from *Carmina Gadelica* by Alexander Carmichael (Scottish Academic Press, Edinburgh, 1971). Reprinted by permission of Scottish Academic Press Ltd

p. 25: St Francis of Assisi, 'Lord, make me an instrument . . .' from *God of a Hundred Names*, ed. Barbara Greene and Victor Gollancz (Gollancz, London, 1962)
Thomas à Kempis, *The Imitation of Christ*, trans. R. Dudley (Anthony Clarke, Wheathampstead, 1980)

p. 26: Edward Hays, 'Autumn Psalm of Fearlessness' from *Prayers for a Planetary Pilgrim* (Forest of Peace Books, Leavenworth, KS, 1989). Reprinted by permission of Forest of Peace Books Inc.

p. 28: Anthony Duncan, 'A Litany for Peace'. Reprinted by permission of the author

p. 29: Pseudo-Augustine, 'Lord, put thou my tears . . .' from *A Book of Peace*, ed. Elizabeth Goudge (Michael Joseph, London, 1967)

Cardinal Newman, 'Prayer for Peace of Heart' from *Everyday Prayer Book*, ed. Dermot Hurley (Geoffrey Chapman, London, 1974)

p. 30: Miriam Therese Winter, 'A Psalm of Benediction' from *Womanword* (Crossroad, New York, 1991). Copyright © 1990 by Medical Mission Sisters

p. 31: Alice A. Bailey, 'The Affirmation of the Disciple' from *Telepathy and the Etheric Vehicle* (The Lucis Press, London), p. 197. Reprinted by permission of the Lucis Trust Ltd

p. 32: Mary Rogers, 'Deep peace of the running wave...' from *Earth Prayers*, ed. E. Roberts and E. Amidon (HarperCollins, New York, 1991). Copyright © 1991 by Elizabeth Roberts and E. Amidon. Reprinted by permission of HarperCollins Publishers

p. 33: Traditional Gaelic, 'The peace of God...' from *Carmina Gadelica* by Alexander Carmichael (Scottish Academic Press, Edinburgh, 1971). Reprinted by permission of Scottish Academic Press Ltd
Traditional Irish, 'May the blessing...' from *Carmina Gadelica* by Alexander Cramichael (Scottish Academic Press, Edinburgh, 1971). By permission of the publishers

p. 34: Traditional Gaelic, 'Peace between neighbours...' from *Carmina Gadelica* by Alexander Carmichael (Scottish Academic Press, Edinburgh, 1971). By permission of the publishers
Traditional Gaelic, 'The peace of joys...' from *Carmina Gadelica* by Alexander Carmichael (Scottish Academic Press, Edinburgh, 1971). By permission of the publishers

p. 35: Traditional Gaelic, 'Blessing for a House' from *Carmina Gadelica* by Alexander Carmichael (Scottish Academic Press, Edinburgh, 1971). By permission of the publishers

pp. 36–39. 'The Vision of Enoch' from *The Gospel of the Essenes*, trans. Edmond Bordeaux Szekely (C. W. Daniel & Co., London, 1974)

p. 40: Alice A. Bailey, *Discipleship in the New Age* (The Lucis Press, London), Vol. II, p. 642. Reprinted by permission of the Lucis Trust Ltd

p. 41: Edward Hays, 'A Benediction at the End of a Prayer Time' from *Prayers for a Planetary Pilgrim* (Forest of Peace Books, Leavenworth, KS, 1989). Reprinted by permission of Forest of Peace Books Inc.

p. 42: José Arguëlles, 'Prayer of the Seven Galactic Directions' from *Surfers of the Zuvuya*, copyright © 1989 José Arguëlles. Reprinted by permission of Bear & Co. Inc., PO Drawer 2860, Sante Fe, NM 87504

p. 43: 'Alî (ibn Abû Tâlib), 'Silence is the garden of meditation...' from *Maxims of 'Alî* (Ashraf Publications, Lahore, n.d.)
'Better than a thousand...', *Dhammapada*, from *Sacred Books of the*

East, trans. Max Muller (Clarendon Press, Oxford, 1989), Vol. x. Reprinted by permission of Oxford University Press

Swami Sivananda, *The Practice of Meditation* (Ali Michel, Paris, 1950)

p. 45: Philip le Galoise, 'The stillness of a stone . . .' Reprinted by permission of the author

Caitlín Matthews, 'Let us not demonise . . .' Reprinted by permission of the author

John Matthews, 'The Dream of peace . . .' Reprinted by permission of the author

p. 46: Robert Fuller, 'I see the possibility . . .' from an interview in *At the Leading Edge*, ed. Michael Toms (Larson Publications, New York, 1991)

'God is peace . . .', *Zohan* from *Major Trends in Jewish Mysticism*, trans. G. Scholem (Schocken Books, New York, 1954)

The Dhammapada, trans. Juan Mascaro (Penguin Classics, London, 1973). Copyright © Juan Mascaro, 1973. Reprinted by permission of Penguin Books Ltd

Anon., 'Contest of Homer and Hesiod' from *Spiritual Authority and Temporal Power in the Indian Theory of Government* by Ananda Coomerswamy (American Oriental Society, New Haven, Conn., 1942)

p. 47: Dante Alighieri, *De monarchia*, IV from *Dante's Latin Works*, trans. A. G. Ferrers Howell and P. H. Wicksteed (Temple Classics, London, 1904–40)

Brihad-Aranyaka Upanishad, IV.iv.23 from *The Thirteen Principal Upanishads*, trans. Robert E. Hume (Oxford University Press, London, 1921–34). Reprinted by permission of Oxford University Press

Swami Ramdas, 'Peace is in the heart . . .' from *The Vision* (Kanhangad, 1954)

Swami Sivananda, 'A peaceful mind . . .' from *Japa Yoga* (Yoga-Vedanta Forest University, Rishikesh, India, 1952)

Meister Eckhart, 'There is nowhere perfect . . .' from *Meister Eckhart: A Modern Translation* by R. B. Blakney (Harper & Bros., New York, 1941)

p. 48: *Qur'ân*, xiii.82 from *The Glorious Qur'ân*, trans. Marmaduke Pichthall (Government Central Press, Hyderabad, 1938)

Dame Julian of Norwich, *Revelations of Divine Love*, ed. Grace Warrack (Methuen & Co., London, 1901–52). Reprinted by permission of the publishers

Helen Suso, 'In peace . . .' from *The Little Book of Eternal Wisdom*, trans. J. M. Clarke (Faber & Faber, London, 1953)

John Smith the Platonist, *Select Discourses* (London, 1821)

Chuang-tse, 'Take no heed . . .' from *Mystic Moralist and Social*

Reformer, trans. H. A. Giles (Quarto, London, 1889)
Muhammad, *The Sayings of Muhammad*, comp. Sir A. Suhrawardy
(John Murray, London, 1941)

p. 49: Swami Ramdas, 'We try to acquire . . .' from *The Vision*
(Kanhangad, 1954)
St Augustine, *The City of God*, trans. J. Healy (Everyman, London
and New York, 1945)
Rabbi Bunam, 'Our sages say: "Seek peace in your own place . . ."'
from *Forms of Prayer*, Vol. I, Daily and Sabbath Prayerbook (Reform
Synagogues of Great Britain, London, 1977). Reprinted by permission
The Dhammapada, trans. Juan Mascaro (Penguin Classics, London,
1973). Copyright © Juan Mascaro, 1973. Reprinted by permission of
Penguin Books Ltd

p. 50: Dionysius the Areopagite, 'All things in motion . . .' from *On the
Divine Names and the Mystical Theology*, trans. C. E. Rolt (Society for
Promoting Christian Knowledge, London, 1920–40)
Swami Ramdas, *Guide to the Aspirants* (Anandashram Series No. 13,
Kanhanged, 1949)
Alice A. Bailey, *Discipleship in the New Age* (The Lucis Press,
London), Vol. II, p. 321. Reprinted by permission of the Lucis Trust
Philo, *Works*, trans. F. H. Colson (Loeb Classics, Phaidon Press,
Oxford, 1946)

p. 51: Lao Tzu *Tao Te Ching*, trans. D. C. Lau (Penguin Classics,
London, 1963), II.lxxix.190–92. Copyright © D. C. Lau, 1963.
Reprinted by permission of Penguin Books Ltd
Black Elk, *The Sacred Pipe: Black Elk's Account of the Seven Rites of
the Oglala Sioux*, ed. Joseph Epes Brown (Penguin Books, London,
1971). Copyright © 1953 by the University of Oklahoma Press.
Reprinted by permission of University of Oklahoma Press
William Law, *The Selected Mystical Writings of William Law*, ed. S.
Hobhouse (Rockliffe, London, 1938–49)

p. 52: Meister Eckhart, 'All Gods wants of man . . .' from *Meister
Eckhart* by F. Pfieffer, trans. C. de B. Evans (Element Books,
Shaftesbury, 1989)
John Tauler, *Life and Sermons of Dr John Tauler*, trans. Susanna
Whiskworth (New York, 1858)
Qur'ân, xv.45–9 frm *The Glorious Qur'ân*, trans. Marmaduke
Pichthall (Government Central Press, Hyderabad, 1938)
Sister Consolata, *Un Appel de Christ au monde*, trans. unknown
(Editions S. Canisius, Fribourg, n.d.)

p. 53: Plotinus, *The Enneads*, trans. Stephen Mackenna (Faber & Faber,
London, 1956)
Alice A. Bailey, *Discipleship in the New Age* (The Lucis Press,

London), Vol.ii, p. 245. Reprinted by permission of the Lucis Trust Ltd
Hermes Trismegistus, *Hermetica*, ed. and trans. Walter Scott
(Clarendon Press, Oxford, 1924–36). Reprinted by permission of
Oxford University Press

p. 54: Ananda Moyî, *Sat-Bani*, trans. H. R. Joshi Calentter (Chatterjee,
Chuckervertly, 1940)
　Søren Kierkegaard, 'To thee, O God . . .' from *A Book of Peace*, ed.
Elizabeth Goudge (Michael Joseph, London, 1967)
　Thomas Fuller, 'Give peace, that is . . .' from *A Book of Peace*, ed.
Elizabeth Goudge (Michael Joseph, London, 1967)

p. 55: Alice A. Bailey, *Discipleship in the New Age* (The Lucis Press,
London), Vol. ii, p. 664. Reprinted by permission of the Lucis Trust Ltd
　Hadewijch of Brabent, 'The Service of Love', trans. Oliver Davies,
from *Beguine Spirituality*, ed. Fiona Bowie (Society for Promoting
Christian Knowledge, London, 1989)
　John Redtail Freesoul, *Breath of the Invisible* (Quest Books, Wheaton,
Illinois, 1986). Reprinted by permission of Theosophical Publishing
House

p. 56: Anon., *Vishnu Purana*, trans. W. H. Wilson (London, 1840)

p. 58: William Anderson, 'Incantation'. 'Reprinted by permission of the
author
　'The Song of the Harper' form *The Wisdom of the Ancient Egyptians*
by William MacQuitty (Sheldon Press, London, 1978). Reprinted by
permission of the publishers

p. 59: Moyra Caldecott, 'Christmas List'. Reprinted by permission of
the author

p. 60: O. V. de L. Milosz, 'Psalm of the King of Beauty', trans. Edouard
Roditi, from *The Noble Traveller: The Life and Writings of O. V. de L.
Milosz*, ed. Christopher Bamford (Lindisfarne Press, 1985). Reprinted by
permission of Lindisfarne Press, RR4 Box 94 A 1, Hudson, NY 125324,
USA (available in the UK from Element Books)

p. 61: Dolores Ashcroft-Nowicki, 'Misunderstanding'. Reprinted by
permission of the author

p. 62: Wolfe van Brussel, 'The Horsewoman'. Reprinted by permission
of the athuor

p. 63: 'War God's Horse Song I', words by Tall Kia ahni, interpreted by
Louis Watchman, from *Technicians of the Sacred*. Second edition,
revised and expanded, by Jerome Rothenberg (University of California
Press, Berkeley, 1985). Copyright © 1968, 1985, Jerome Rothenberg.
Reprinted by permission of University of California Press

p. 64: David Cloutier, 'Song to Quiet the Ocean' from *Spirit Spirit: Shaman Songs*. Copyright © 1980 by David Cloutier. Reprinted by permission of Copper Beech Press, Box 1852, Brown University, Providence, RI 02912, USA

p. 65: John Matthews, 'Praying to the World'. Reprinted by permission of the author

p. 66: Gerard Manley Hopkins, 'Peace' from *Selected Poems of Gerard Manley Hopkins*, ed. James Reeves (Heinemann, London, 1953)

p. 67: Kathleen Raine, 'Autumnal'. Reprinted by permission of the author

p. 68: 'Yucatec-Maya Song' from *Native Mesoamerican Spirituality*, ed. and trans. Miguel Leon-Portilla (Paulist Press, New York/Society for Promoting Christian Knowledge, London, 1980). Copyright © 1980 by The Missionary Society of St Paul the Apostle in the State of New York. Reprinted by permission of Paulist Press and Society for Promoting Christian Knowledge

p. 69: 'The Rain Cloud', *Lotus Sutra* from *Only One Earth* (United Nations Environmental Sabbath Day Project, New York, n.d.)

pp. 70–1: George Herbert, 'Resurrection' from *A Book of Peace*, ed. Elizabeth Goudge (Michael Joseph, London, 1967)

pp. 72–5: Caitlín Matthews, 'Into the Peace of Sophia'. Reprinted by permission of the author

pp. 76 and 79: St Hildegard of Bingen, 'Sequence for the Holy Spirit' and 'Responsory for the Holy Innocents' from *Symphonica by St. Hildegard of Bingen*, trans. Barbara Newman (Cornell University Press, Cornell, 1988)

p. 77: Kathleen Raine, 'Suddenly it was as if . . .' Reprinted by permission of the author

p. 78: John Clare, 'Peace' from *A Book of Peace*, ed. Elizabeth Goudge (Michael Joseph, London, 1967)
    Peter Russell, 'Poem for Peace: Black-headed Gulls on the Thames' from *All for the Wolves: Selected Poems 1947–1975*, ed. Peter Jay (Anvill Press Poetry, London, 1984). Reprinted by permission of the publishers

p. 79: Kathleen Raine, 'After Hearing a Tape-recording of Music by Mechtilde of Magdeburg'. Reprinted by permission of the author

p. 80: Darrell Figgis, 'Anach' from *Lyra Celtica* by E. A. Sharp (Patrick Geddes, Edinburgh, 1896)

p. 81: William Blake, 'The Divine Image' from *Complete Prose and*

Poetry of William Blake, ed. G. Keynes (The Nonesuch Press, London, 1975)

pp. 82 and 83: John-Francis Phipps, 'The Inner Essence of Peace' and 'The Guru and the Politician'. Reprinted by permission of the author

pp. 84–5: Dolores Ashcroft-Nowicki, 'The Song of the Five Sisters'. Reprinted by permission of the author

p. 85: Moyra Caldecott, 'Our Planet's Death'. Reprinted by permission of the author
Wendell Berry, 'The Peace of Wild Things' from *Openings* (Harcourt Brace Jovanovich Inc., New York, 1968)

p. 86: Mary Oliver, 'Sleeping in the Forest' from *Twelve Moons* (Little, Brown & Co., Boston, 1979)

p. 87: Charles Simic, 'Stone' from *Dismantling the Silence* (George Braziller Inc., New York, 1971)

p. 88: Emily Brontë, 'The Prisoner' from *The Complete Poems of Emily, Jane and Anne Brontë*, ed. Wise and Symington (Shakespeare Head Press, Oxford, 1934)

p. 89: Samuel Speed, 'Peace' from *A Book of Peace*, ed. Elizabeth Goudge (Michael Joseph, London, 1967)

p. 90: Edwin Muir, 'Sunset', *Collected Poems of Edwin Muir* (Faber & Faber, London). Copyright © 1960 by Willa Muir by permission of Faber & Faber Ltd and Oxford University Press Inc., New York
Peter Russell, 'Love is Not Something You Do'. Reprinted by permission of the author

p. 91: Gary Snyder, 'For the Children' from *Turtle Island* by Gary Snyder. Copyright © 1974 by Gary Snyder. Reprinted by permission of New Directions Publishing Corporation, New York City

pp. 94–5: O. V. de L. Milosz, 'Psalm of Reintegration', trans. Edouard Roditi, from *The Noble Traveller: The Life and Writings of O. V. de L. Milosz*, ed. Christopher Bamford (Lindisfarne Press, 1985). Reprinted by permission of Lindisfarne Press, RR4 Box 94 A 1, Hudson, NY 125324, USA (available in the UK from Element Books)

p. 96: W. H. Davies, 'Peace and Rest' from *The Complete Poems of W. H. Davies* (Jonathan Cape, London, n.d.)

p. 97: Nancy Wood, 'It is our quiet time . . .' from *Hollering Sun* (Simon & Schuster, New York, 1972)

pp. 98–99: Miriam Therese Winter, 'Sing of a Blessing' (words and music) from *Womansong*. Copyright © Medical Mission Sisters, 1987. Reprinted by permission of copyright owner

p. 100: 'Let Us Enjoy Ourselves Here and Now' from *Native Mesoamerican Spirituality*, ed. and trans. Miguel Leon-Portilla (Paulist Press, New York Society for Promoting Christian Knowledge, London, 1980). Copyright © 1980 by The Missionary Society of St Paul the Apostle in the State of New York. Reprinted by permission of Paulist Press and Society for Promoting Christian Knowledge

p. 101: Traditional Gaelic, 'Chant of Peace' from *Carmina Gadelica* by Alexander Carmichael (Scottish Academic Press, Edinburgh, 1971). Reprinted by permission of Scottish Academic Press Ltd

pp. 102–3. Dolores Ashcroft-Nowicki, 'The Return'. Reprinted by permission of the author

p. 103: Jan Nation, 'Who are the Peacemakers?' Reprinted by permission of the author

p. 104: Miriam Therese Winter, 'Blessing Song' (words and music) from *Womansong*. Copyright © Medical Mission Sisters, 1987. Reprinted by permission of copyright owner

p. 105: Confucius, 'If one only understood . . .' from *The Wisdom of Confucius* by Ling Yutang (Modern Library, New York, 1938)
St Gregory of Sinai, 'A ship has no need . . .' from *Writings from the Philokalia on Prayer of the Heart*, trans. E. Kadloubovsky and E. E. H. Palmer (Faber & Faber, London, 1951)

p. 107: Black Elk, *The Sacred Pipe: Black Elk's Account of the Seven Rites of the Oglala Sioux*, ed. Joseph Epes Brown (Penguin Books, London, 1971). Copyright © 1953 by the University of Oklahoma Press. Reprinted by permission of Oklahoma University Press

pp. 108–10: David Spangler, 'A Prayer for Peace'. Reprinted by permission of the author

pp. 110–23: 'The Sevenfold Peace', *The Essene Book of Jesus* from *The Gospel of the Essenes*, trans. Edmond Bordeaux Szekely (C. W. Daniel & Co., London, 1974)

pp. 124–5: Anon., 'The Bodhisattva Vow' from *Maintaining the Bodhisattva Vow* (Kagyou Droder Kunchab, San Francisco, 1984)

p. 126: Brooke Medecine Eagle, 'Ceremony of Peace'. Reprinted by permission of the author

p. 127: Aurora Terrenus (Holy Order of Wisdom), 'In Lighting the Candle'/'In Extinguishing the Candle'. Reprinted by permission of the author

pp. 128–31: R. J. Stewart, 'The Weaver's Song'. Reprinted by permission of the author

p. 132: Geraint ap Iorwerth (Order of Sancta Sophia), 'Honouring the Divine Wisdom: Challenging Humanity to Follow The Way'. Reprinted by permission of the author

p. 133: Stuart Littlejohn, 'Pax Deae: The Peace of the Goddess'. Reprinted by permission of the author

pp. 134–5: Felicity Wombwell, 'A Ceremony of Peace'. Reprinted by permission of the author

p. 136: Naomi Ozaniec, 'Tread the inner spiral . . .' Reprinted by permission of the author

p. 137: Sir George Trevelyan, 'The Inner Chamber of Peace'. Reprinted by permission of the author

pp. 135–39: Philip le Galoise, 'Victory: A Question and an Answer'. Reprinted by permission of the author

pp. 140–1: F. C. Happold, Prayer and Meditation (Penguin Books, London, 1971). Copyright © F. C. Happold, 1971. Reprinted by permission of Penguin Books Ltd

p. 142: Lama Shereb Gyaltsen Amipa, 'Absolute Bodhicitta', The Opening of the Lotus (Wisdom Publications, Boston, MA, 1987)

p. 143: Seren Wildwood, 'Ritual of Reconciliation'. Reprinted by permission of the author

pp. 144–5: Diana Paxson, 'Binding the Wolf: A Peace Ritual in the Norse Tradition'. Reprinted by permission of the author

p. 146–7: Olivia Robertson, Priestess Hierophant (Fellowship of Isis), 'Peace of the Mother God: Rainbow Network of the Fellowship of Isis'. Reprinted by permission of the author

pp. 149–5: Caitlín Matthews, 'Self-clarification and the Resolution of the Conflict'. Reprinted by permission of the author

pp. 152–3: Bishop Ignatii, 'How to Preserve Within You the Peace of God' from The Art of Prayer: An Orthodox Anthology by I. Chariton, ed. Timothy Ware (Faber & Faber, London, 1966). By permission of the publishers

pp. 154–6: Michael Beechey, 'A Dream of Peace: A Visualisation'. Reprinted by permission of the author

p. 157: Al-Ghazali, 'At death . . . [we are] separated . . .' from Readings from the Mystics of Islam by Margaret Smith (Lusac, London, 1950)
     Richard of Saint-Victor, 'This is the invocation . . .' from Richard of Saint-Victor, trans. Clare Kirchenberger (Faber & Faber, London, 1957)

p. 158: Isidorus, 'A Prayer for Peace' (from the Greek: inscription from

Medinet Madi, Egypt: P. M. Fraser, Ptolemaic Alexandria, ii.960f), *Hymn to Isis*, trans. T. du Quesne. Reprinted by permission of the translator

p. 159: Alice A. Bailey, 'The Great Invocation' from *Discipleship in the New Age* (The Lucis Press, London), Vol. ii, pp. 157–8. Reprinted by permission of the Lucis Trust Ltd

pp. 160–2 Gareth Knight, 'Invocation of the Angels of the Spheres and the Prince of Peace for the Healing of the World'. Reprinted by permission of the author

p. 163: Fifth-century Irish, 'The Song of Long Life', trans. Kuno Meyer from *Learning in Ireland in the Fifth Century and the Transmission of Letters (School of Irish Learning, 1913)*
Alice A. Bailey, *The Externalisation of the Hierarchy* (The Lucis Press, London), p. 144. Reprinted by permission of the Lucis Trust Ltd

p. 164: Helene Hess and Ken Mills, 'Earth Spirit Invocation'. Reprinted by permission of the authors

p. 165: Edward Hays, 'Advent Peace Psalm' from *Prayers for a Planetary Pilgrim* (Forest of Peace Books, Leavenworth, KS, 1989). Reprinted by permission of Forest of Peace Books Inc.

p. 166: Hesiod, 'Hymn to Ares' from *The Homeric Hymns and Homerica*, trans. H. G. Evelyn-White (Harvard University Press, Cambridge, Mass., 1974). Reprinted by permission of the publisher and the Loeb Classical Library

p. 167: Alice A. Bailey, *The Externalisation of the Hierarchy* (The Lucis Press, London), p. 249. Reprinted by permission of the Lucis Trust Ltd

p. 168: William Bloom, 'The Glastonbury Invocation'. Reprinted by permission of the author

p. 169: John Matthews, 'Litany of the Gods'. Reprinted by permission of the author

p. 170: Traditional Gaelic, 'O Being of Life!' from *Carmina Gadelica* by Alexander Carmichael (Scottish Academic Press, Edinburgh, 1971). Reprinted by permission of the Scottish Academic Press Ltd

p. 171: 'Petition to Makataeshigun' from *Ojibway Ceremonies* by Basil Johnston (University of Nebraska Press, Lincoln, Nebraska, 1990). Copyright © 1982 by McClelland and Stewart. Reprinted by permission of University of Nebraska Press

p. 172: Anon., 'Go in Peace, Come in Peace' from *The Penguin Book of Hebrew Verse*, trans. T. Carmi (Allen Lane, London, 1981). Copyright © T. Carmi, 1981. Reprinted by permission of Penguin Books Ltd

(Penguin/Arkana Books, London, 1989). Copyright © 1950, 1967 The Bollingen Foundation Incorporated. Reprinted by permission of Penguin Books Ltd and Princeton University Press

p. 188–90: Traditional Iroquois, 'The Roots of Peace' from *I Become Part of It*, ed. D. M. Dooling and Paul Jordan-Smith (Parabola Books, New York, 1989). Reprinted by permission of the publishers

p. 191: Haji Ibrahim of Kerbela, *The Mystic Rose from the Garden of the King*, trans. F. L. Cartwright. Reprinted by permission of Element Books Ltd

p. 192: Kevin Crossley-Holland, 'After Ragnarok' from *A Re-telling of the Norse Myths* (André Deutsch Ltd, London, 1980). Reprinted by permission of the publishers

p. 193: Ann Marie Hancock, 'Mir – A Mirror of Peace in the Sky' from *Be a Light: Miracles of Medjugorje* (The Donning Company/Publishers, Norfolk, USA, 1990)

p. 194: Epictetus, 'Remember that it is not only desire . . .' from *The Stoic and Epicurean Philosophers*, ed. W. J. Oates (Random House, New York, 1940)

Teilhard de Chardin, *Hymn of the Universe* (HarperCollins, London, 1969). Copyright © 1961 by Éditions du Seuil. English translation copyright William Collins Sons & Co. Ltd and Harper & Row, Publishers, Inc. Reprinted by permission of HarperCollins Publishers

p. 195: Haji Ibrahim of Kerbela, *The Mystic Rose from the Garden of the King*, trans F. L. Cartwright. Reprinted by permission of Element Books Ltd

p. 196: Alan Bleakley, 'Aphrodite: Personification of Peace'. Reprinted by permission of the author
Joseph Campbell, *The Inner Reaches of Outer Space* (Alfred van der Marck Editions, New York, 1985)

p. 197: Dame Julian of Norwich, *Revelations of Divine Love*, ed. Grace Warrack (Methuen & Co., London, 1901–52). Reprinted by permission of the publishers

p. 198: 'There lives no man on earth . . .', *Theologia Germanica* from *A Book of Peace*, ed. Elizabeth Goudge (Michael Joseph, London, 1967)

p. 199: Thomas Berry, *The Dream of the Earth* (Sierra Club Books, San Francisco, 1988). Copyright © 1988 by Thomas Berry. Reprinted by permission of Sierra Club Books

p. 200: Beatrice of Nazareth, 'The Power of Love', trans. Oliver Davies, from *Beguine Spirituality*, ed. Fiona Bowie (Society for Promoting Christian Knowledge, London, 1989)

p. 201: Pierre Delattre, *Tales of a Dalai Lama* (Penguin Books, London, 1971)

p. 202: Baba Hari Dass, 'Good is Peace' from *For the Love of Good*, ed. Benjamin Shield and Richard Carlson (New World Library, San Rafael, 1990)

p. 202–3: 'Liberation' from 'The Supreme Teaching', *The Upanishads*, trans. Juan Mascaro (Penguin Classics, London, 1965). Copyright © Juan Mascaro, 1965. Reprinted by permission of Penguin Books Ltd

p. 204: *The Bhagavad Gita*, trans. Juan Mascaro (Penguin Classics, 1962). Copyright © Juan Mascaro, 1962. Reprinted by permission of Penguin Books Ltd

p. 205: Ivan Illich, 'Peace is a Way of Life' from *The Best of Resurgence*, ed. John Button (Green Books, Bideford, 1991)
   Mikhail Gorbachev, *Perestroika* (Collins, London, 1987)

INDEX OF FIRST LINES